SHIPS
SHIPWRE
&
MARITIME INCIDENTS

C000171653

---

around the
ISLES OF SCILLY

ISLES OF SCILLY MUSEUM PUBLICATION NO. 3
Revised edition - 1999

A chronological list of incidents, accidents,
shipwrecks and maritime events around the Isles
of Scilly and Seven Stones Reef

edited by Richard Larn

Cover illustration shows the barque *Minnehaha*, of Liverpool,
wrecked on the Jolly Rocks at Peninnis Point, St. Marys. She
drove ashore on Sunday 18 January 1874, in a gale accompanied
by fog, with the loss of her captain, eight crew and a pilot.
Acknowledgment: Frank Gibson

INTRODUCTION

The sea has played a major role in the lives of every Scillonian through-out history, and like all island communities the sea dictates the fortunes of its inhabitants, their way of life, and their very existence. The Isles of Scilly are more remote and disadvantaged than is generally appreciated since, with the exception of the Outer Hebrides, even people living in the island groups off the coast of Scotland such as the Inner Hebrides, Orkney and Shetlands, live on larger islands, in or close to larger towns or the mainland, and enjoy better facilities, services and subsidised transport.

The short accounts of ships, shipwrecks and maritime events which follow in chronological order are but a snapshot of life in the Isles of Scilly since the 14th century. No events prior to 1305 are known, and up until the early 1600's details of what happened at sea round the islands are scarce. Through it all runs a golden thread of heroism and resourceful-ness. Many feats of rescue, salvage and self-sacrifice were performed by the islanders. True, they were always glad of a chance to augment their incomes from the salvageable flotsam, jetsam and lagan, but the saving of human life was, and still is, a priority. Life on these islands was often pre-carious and hard, but there is no evidence that deliberate organised wreck-ing was carried out here, or for that matter on mainland Cornwall, despite lurid tales to the contrary.

The islands present a formidable obstacle at the junction of the Bristol, English and St. George's Channels. Low lying, twenty-four miles out into the Atlantic, often shrouded in fog, with hundreds of jagged rocks lurking just below the surface, they have claimed over a thousand ships of all types and nationalities. No doubt somewhere amongst the islands are the remains of a Phoenician trader, a Roman galley, a Viking longboat or even a Barbary pirate ship, since these and others more ancient must, by inference from our historical knowledge, have visited, raided or been based here at some time.

Other island communities, such as those in Scotland, have oral legends and traditions passed down from generation to generation for nigh on 2,000 years. In Scilly, due to famine, war, disease, absentee landlords and de-population, little such tradition survives. Even the old parish records for Scilly, often a prolific source of information concerning shipwrecks, have been lost due to a fire in 1751. There does remain however, the remote possibility that some record of the early years may yet survive somewhere on the mainland, Troutbeck having used information from them in his writing in 1790. A steady flow of new historic information arrives at the islands' Museum from not only the mainland, but world wide. Often in the form of new publications, whose authors have diligently researched some aspect of Scillonian history, it is obvious there is a vast amount of material scattered amongst the archives and newspapers of Gt. Britain. On the very edge of the 21st century, as we enter further into the age of communication technology, the islands can only benefit from an increase in this academic mainland input, enriching our knowledge of the past.

Underwater exploration by divers amongst the islands often poses a problem in reverse, when the physical remains of an unknown shipwreck are found but no documentary record of its loss exists. In such cases survey and excavation may offer the only hope of identification. Literally a sea-mount, the Isles of Scilly rise to the surface from deep water, and until recently exploration of the seabed has been limited to safe air diving depths of around 50-60m(165-196ft). Today, technology in the form of mixed-gas and Nitrox diving, remote controlled cameras and exploration vehicles, greatly extend previous depth limitations for sport diving. Future exploration of the deep sea that surrounds Scilly offers not only the possibility of many new and exciting underwater finds, but the almost certain prospect of intact historic shipwrecks being located. Richard Larn. 1999.

Acknowledgements

The Isles of Scilly Museum is indebted to Richard Larn for his editing of this revised millennium edition, as well as his contribution to three previous editions; also to Frank Gibson and David McBride for allowing use of photographs from their collections. We wish to thank Roy Graham for permission to reuse some of his introduction to the 1988 edition; the late John Pickwell, who edited it, and Len Michell for proof reading this revised edition. Other contributors include John Davies, of Truro; Molly Mortimer, of London and the late Frank Dunn, of the Lizard, Cornwall. We also acknowledge Charlotte Dorrien Smith, who compiled the first published Scilly shipwreck list forty year ago, which appeared in the 1959 edition of the 'Mariner's Mirror,' the journal of the Society for Nautical Research.

BIBLIOGRAPHY

The following is a list of major publications relating to shipwrecks and the maritime history of Scilly, most if not all of which are to be found in the Isles of Scilly Museum reference library, St.Mary's. The more recent ones are available through many of the island's book sellers.

A CENTURY OF IMAGES. Cowan, R. 1997. Andre Deutsch Ltd. London. ISBN 0-233-98992-7

ADMIRAL SHOVELL's TREASURE – IN THE ISLES OF SCILLY. McBride, P. & Larn, R. 1999. Shipwreck & Marine. ISBN 0-9523971-2-9 & 3-7

A NATURAL & HISTORICAL ACCOUNT OF THE ISLANDS OF SCILLY. Heath, R. 1750(1967 edition) ISBN 900409-01-0

A SEA MISCELLANY OF CORNWALL & THE ISLES OF SCILLY. Gillis, R. 1968. Harvey Barton, Bristol.

AUGUSTUS SMITH OF SCILLY. Inglis-Jones, E.1969. Faber & Faber, London. ISBN 571-08695-0

A YACHTSMAN GUIDE TO SCILLY. Gooding, J. c1986. ISBN 0-907205-00-3

BISHOP ROCK – lighthouses of England & Wales. Boyle, M. 1997.
B.&T.Publications.
ISBN 1-901043-05-3

CASTAWAY & WRECKED. Cowan, R. 1978. Duckworth & Co Ltd., London.
ISBN 0-7156-1145-3

CORNWALL'S EARLY LIFEBOATS. Noall, C. 1989. Tor Mark
Press, Penryn. ISBN 0-85025-317-9

CORNISH LIGHTS & SHIPWRECKS. Noall, C. 1968. Bradford
Barton, Truro.

CORNISH SHIPWRECKS, Vol. 3. Larn, R. 1971. David & Charles,
Newton Abbot. ISBN 0-7153-4976-7

CORNISH SHIPWRECKS ILLUSTRATED. Noall, C. & Farr, G.

CORNWALL's LIGHTHOUSE HERITAGE. Tarrant, M. 1990.
Twelveheads Press, Truro.
ISBN 0-906294-20-7

DEEP SEA TREASURE. Williams, M. 1981. William Heinemann
Ltd. ISBN 434-866660-1

EXCAVATION OF HMS. ASSOCIATION. Rogers, R. 1970.
Lyonesse Publications, Scilly.

EXPLORATION OF A DROWNED LANDSCAPE. Thomas, C.
1985. B. T. Batsford Ltd,
London. ISBN 0-7134-4852-0

EXPLORING UNDERWATER THE ISLES OF SCILLY. Groves,
M. 1988. Porth Books.
ISBN 0-9510297-11

GIG RACING IN THE ISLES OF SCILLY. Gibson, F. c1985.
Private publication

GIGS & CUTTERS OF THE ISLES OF SCILLY. Jenkins, A.
1975. Private publication.

HMS. ASSOCIATION - SANK 1707. Mace, M. 1982. Scillonian
Diving Services.

HMS. COLOSSUS. Morris, R. 1979. Hutchinson, London.
ISBN 0-09-134660-6

ISLAND CAMERA. Arlott, J. 1972 & '83. David & Charles,
Newton Abbot.
ISBN 0-7153-8391-4

ISLES OF FLOWERS. Kay, E. 1963. Alvin Redman,
London.

MY ISLAND WAR. - recollections of a WREN. Williams, M. 1990.
Private publication.
ISBN 0-9515206-0-1

SCILLONIAN WAR DIARY. 1914-1918. Vol. 1-3. Osborne, J. 1990.
Private publication, Isles of Scilly.

SCILLONIAN WAR DIARY. 1939-1945. Vol. 1-4. Osborne, J. 1990.
Private publication, Isles of Scilly.

SHIPWRECK. Fowles, J. 1974. Jonathan Cape Ltd., London.
ISBN 0-224-01053-0

SHIPWRECK INDEX OF THE BRITISH ISLES. Vol.1. Larn, R. &
B. 1995. Lloyd's Register of
Shipping, London.
ISBN 0900528-88-5

SHIPWRECKS ON THE ISLES OF SCILLY. Gibson, F.E. 1967.
Private publication, Isles of Scilly

SHIPWRECKS OF THE ISLES OF SCILLY. Larn, R. 1992.
Thomas & Lochar.
ISBN 0-946537-84-4

SUNKEN TREASURE.   Morris, R. 1975.
Private publication.

SUNKEN TREASURE.   Williams, M.1980. Cassell Ltd.,
London. ISBN 0-304-30502-2

TALES OF THE CORNISH WRECKERS. Vivian, J. 1969. Tor
Press, Truro

THE CITA.   Larn, R. & McBride, D. 1998.
Shipwreck & Marine,
ISBN 0-9523971-1-0

THE FORTUNATE ISLANDS. Bowley, R. 8th ed. 1990.
Bowley Publications Ltd. St.
Mary's. Isles of Scilly

THE ISLES OF SCILLY.   Over, L. 1993. Phillimore,
Chichester.
ISBN 085033-884-0

THE ISLES OF SCILLY EYE WITNESS 1958-1984. Gibson, F.
1985. Private publication.

THE LOST LAND.   Dunbar, J. 1958. Collins, London

THE PILOT GIGS OF CORNWALL & THE ISLES OF SCILLY
Gillis, R. 1978. Isles of Scilly
Museum publication No.5

THE SAVAGE SEA.   Gibson, F. St. Mary's. 1987

THE SCILLONIAN.   Bi-annual magazine of the Isles of
Scilly.1925 - to date. Mumford, C.
St. Mary's

THE SCILLONIAN AND HIS BOAT, Jenkins, A. 1982.
Private publication.
ISBN 0-9508017-0-4

THE SHIPWRECK OF SIR CLOUDESLEY SHOVELL. Cooke, J.
1883. John Bellows, Gloucester. Isles
of Scilly Museum publication No.6
WOLF ROCK – lighthouses of England & Wales. Boyle, M.
B.& T. Publications. 1997.
ISBN 1-901043-07-X
WRECK AND RESCUE ROUND THE CORNISH COAST, Vol.2.
Noall, C. & Farr, G. 1965. Bradford
Barton Ltd., Truro
WRECKS AROUND THE CORNISH COAST. Gillis, R. 1968.
Harvey Barton , Truro
WRECKS OF THE ISLES OF SCILLY. du Boulay, J. 1961.
The Mariner's Mirror, reprint, Vol.45
No.4, 12.1959 & Vol.46, No.2, May
1960.

PHOTOGRAPHS - Copies of photographs of shipwrecks in Scilly and West Cornwall are obtainable from Gibson-Kyne Gift Shop, Garrison Lane, St. Mary's, IOS. Tel: 01720-423081.

INFORMATION - Enquiries concerning general Isles of Scilly history, the Museum or shipwrecks, should be addressed to:-
The Curator, Isles of Scilly Museum, Church Street, St. Mary's, IOS. TR21 0JT.
Telephone No; 01720 - 422337

SHIPS,
SHIPWRECKS
& MARITIME INCIDENTS
around the
ISLES OF SCILLY

- in chronological order -

1305 - William le Poer, Coroner of the Isles of Scilly, was imprisoned and held to ransom when he went to Tresco to take charge of wreck cargo. A shipwreck occurred on the Island of Annet at about the same time.

1320 - A vessel of Normandy, from Bordeaux for Dieppe with wine valued at 200 marks and other cargo belonging to merchants of Gascony, was driven by the wind to Scilly where she was boarded, her crew killed and her cargo taken to Falmouth and Fowey.

1342-45 - The cargo and materials of three vessels wrecked during this four year period was plundered by Scillonians much to the annoyance of the Black Prince, who owned the Right of Wreck.

1354 - *Seinte Marie de Coronade,* of Genoa, Anthony de Compaignon owner, was boarded at night in Scilly and the vessel confiscated for non-payment of Custom dues incurred in Brittany.

1375 - *Grace Dieux, Trinitee, Gabriel* and other armed Bristol vessels captured a barge at Scilly.

1382 - A barge of Normandy was captured at Scilly.

1460 - *Marie*, master Hermann Taillour, from Bordeaux to Bristol with merchandise valued at £2,713.13s.4d, was seized at Scilly by two vessels equipped for war, the *Peter Courtenay*, Sir Hugh Courtenay owner, and the *Galiot*, and taken to Fowey.

c1542 - Cannon, artefacts, lead ingots and hundreds of bronze bell fragments, as well as silver coins of Ferdinand & Isabella (1474-1504) and Emperor Charles (1521-55) of Spain found on Bartholomew Ledge, indicate a small Spanish cargo vessel, possibly from Amsterdam to Spain. A single thaler coin of 1555 suggests the wreck was of this period or slightly later. The site was Designated as a Protected Wreck from 3 October 1980.

c1593 – A Spanish vessel was wrecked on Black Rock, Pednathise Head. Local divers found her remains in 1995, including iron cannon, a broken astrolabe bearing a date, some 200 four escudo gold coins, one English and one French silver coin and other items in 50-70m(164-230ft) depth.

1599 - *Advice*, man o'war, was lost off Scilly. This may be the nine gun, 49-61 ton warship built for the Navy at Woolwich in 1586.

1616/17 - One of the vessels equipped by Sir Walter Raleigh to seek gold in Guiana, sank off Scilly during a gale.

1617 - November or December. *Supply,* captain John Totten, with a crew of fifty, an English East Indiaman described as a 'pinnace', homeward bound, drove ashore amongst the Western Rocks, crew and cargo saved; eventually refloated since she made a second voyage to Java in 1621, being laid up in 1623.

1623 - *Angel,* of London, John Duffe master and owner, from Ireland to Rochester, was wrecked.

1635/36 - *Gift of God,* of Kirkcaldy, from London to Bristol, was wrecked off Scilly. The merchants concerned with her cargo included

Edward Forde, of St. Mary, Aldermanbury; Thomas Burnell, St. Olave; and Peter Jones, St. Andrew Undershaft, all of London.

1636 - October. A vessel on passage to Scilly was taken by pirates.

1639 - *Swann,* of Topsham, was attacked near Scilly by two Turkish men o'war but escaped by running ashore. The *Dorothy,* of Dartmouth, 80 tons, was taken near Scilly by the Turks.

1645 - July. A Royalist vessel under the command of captain J. Mucknell, was reported 'run ashore at Scilly and I think will never get off more hereafter', following an indecisive engagement with three Parliamentarian ships. She was almost certainly the *John,* 40 guns, about 500 tons, with which Mucknell had been harrying Parliamentarian shipping only the previous month. It is possible that she was beached intentionally for repairs, having 'received many shot which must do him much harm'.

c1650 - *Royal James,* A Royalist privateer, 28 guns, 250 tons, captain Richard Beach, was captured near Scilly by Parliamentarians. She subsequently served under the Commonwealth government as the *Sorlings.*

1651 -10 May. Two of the Royalists' best frigates 'which rode under the Hugh Hill, near their shore, to prevent our boats coming in to land there', drove ashore in a storm. (The Royalists surrendered on 1 June 1651).

1653 - January. The Penzance-Isles of Scilly packet vessel was taken by a Dutch privateer.

1654 - A vessel was chased ashore on Scilly.
 Primrose, captain Sherwin, was in search of two Spanish frigates which had taken a Bristol bound vessel. While captain Sherwin was on board the *Mayflower* to discuss replacement of his damaged maintopmast, the *Primrose* struck the Seven Stones. She floated off but foundered with the loss of sixteen crew, two women and a child. The survivors were picked up by the *Mayflower* and brought to Scilly, and later taken to Plymouth on board the *Bryher*.

1663 - A vessel from Virginia, 130 tons, was wrecked but her crew were saved.

1665 - 18 January. ***Royal Oak.*** An East Indiaman, captain Robert Lock, built in 1663 on the Thames, was wrecked on the Western Rocks. According to a Mr Daniel, one of the survivors, she struck the Bishop & Clerks, in the Western Rocks. The following is a modernised extract from his account of the wreck:

'Now by what secret cause we know not, on the 18th in the morning before daylight we found ourselves surrounded with rocks and beaches, which terrible sight made us all bestir ourselves, some in the tops to see if there were any passage through but could find none. The crew cast our best bower anchor after cutting our mast away, but all of no avail, the wind being so violent cast our ship between two rocks where she in a quarter of an hour split all in pieces. Some of us miraculously got on the rocks, then day appearing we found ourselves on a low rock that could not preserve us from being washed away at high water, so we ventured upon parts of our ship and got from the rock we first landed on unto a higher rock that praised be God did not overflow but sheltered us from the raging waves. Here we sadly beheld one another, most of us sorely cut and wounded from the sharpness of the rocks, not having meat, drink, or fire to comfort us and many of us in a manner naked because the better able to swim. We continued in this sad and lamentable condition from the 18th in the morning, till the 20th in the morning, in which time some of our pepper and several pieces of our ship drove on shore to Scilly which signified to the inhabitants that there was some ship cast away about their islands, so they looked out and descried our waste upon the rock where we were preserved. Upon sight thereof, the worthy Major Edward Roscaricke, then chief in Scilly, hastened boats to us who came and took us in and landed us at St. Mary's on the 20th day about noon so that we were about fifty-two hours upon the aforesaid rocks, where we endured so much cold that our legs and hands were so swollen that could but few of us stand. This is a true relation of our sad passage.'

1666 - October. The ***Endeavour*** and several other colliers from Wales were wrecked.

1667 - The prize ship *Little Sun* bilged and her hull was given to Col. Anthony Buller to be broken up for the use of the garrison.

December - *Dover* 100 tons, from Malaga, was lost off Scilly and her crew drowned. A Spanish vessel was wrecked, and a passenger of rank complained of the cruelty of the Scillonian's who left him on a rock for a day or two while they salvaged the goods, although they could have rescued him without risk.

11 December - The *Hind,* captain John Withers, a 6th rate man o'war, 8 gun ketch, built at Wyvenhoe in 1655, 41 feet in length, was lost on the Crim.

1670 - 21 August. 'A great ship has been lost about the Scillies, the after part of a wreck has been found.'

1672 - December. A French vessel for London, with wine and brandy, was cast away at night and her cargo lost.

1673 - 27 November. Two Dutch capers and a Guineaman prize they had taken, were lost off Scilly.

1674 - 30 November. *Revenge,* foundered between Scilly and Land's End, probably on the Seven Stones. All but two of her crew of seventeen were drowned.

1675 - 21 February. A large vessel was wrecked at Scilly, and all but four of the crew drowned.

1677 - November. An English vessel, from Barbados with sugar, was cast away but her crew and most of her cargo was saved.

1679 - A large vessel was lost with all hands on Pednathise Head. Part of the wreckage drifted ashore at Perconger.

1680 - The *Phoenix,* captain Wildy, armed with 30 guns, a homeward bound English East Indiaman, carrying white pepper, cloth and spices valued at £10,177.18s.0d., was lost amongst the Western Rocks, possibly on

Menglow Rock, Smith Sound. At a local sale of wreck goods, a 'Thomas Abney, bought 269 pieces of Peerlongs for £202.8s.1d.' [nb. A type of cloth valued at £202.40]

1681 - December. *Golden Lion*, a Virginian trading vessel was lost on the rocks off St.Agnes. The fire in the recently built St.Agnes lighthouse (30 October) was not lit until after the vessel had struck. The keeper was subsequently found guilty of negligence and of stealing part of the cargo.

1685 - A French schooner struck the Rags and anchored close by. Next morning a St. Agnes boat found her abandoned, the master and crew having landed on St. Mary's. The church on St. Agnes was said to have been built with the salvage money paid for this vessel.

1686 - January/early February. The Dutch East Indiaman *Prinses Maria,* of 1,140 tons, built at Zeeland but owned by the Amsterdam Chamber, from Texel to Batavia with wealthy merchants and a very large quantity of silver specie, foundered near Silver Carn, in the Western Rocks. There were no survivors from her complement of 250. James II sent his Royal yacht and men to recover the treasure and take it back to London. When the Dutch owners requested its return he denied its existence. The wreck was found in 1973 by divers working with Rex Cowan, who recovered many coins.
13 September - In a storm described as 'tempestuous beyond description', in which every vessel in the roadstead put to sea and most were dismasted, a vessel carrying copra drove ashore and became a total wreck.

1689 - 18 November. A transport vessel leaving Scilly struck the Woolpack, finally sinking close to the Old Town Gilstone. Iron cannon from this wreck were found by Royal Navy divers in 1964, one gun being raised and landed at St.Mary's quay.
A vessel from Rochelle with salt was wrecked.

1692 - 21 February. An unidentified transport in convoy, possibly Danish, struck a rock when leaving Scilly and foundered.

1694 - 12 May. *Diligente,* a French man o'war, captain Rene du Gray Trouin, fell in with a squadron of six English ships and, being driven amongst the islands and a good deal mauled, was captured. Trouin was charged with firing at an English ship during an earlier encounter. He was taken to Plymouth and put under close arrest, but escaped with four companions and made his way to Brittany in a small boat.

1700 - A vessel was lost during a violent storm. Many of the crew were drowned, but some scrambled ashore where they remained several days. Eventually, a St. Agnes pilot boat reached them, but capsized during the rescue and nearly all the occupants drowned including two St. Agnes men in the pilot boat.

1707 - 22 October. *Association, Eagle, Romney & Firebrand.* After taking part in the siege of Toulon that year, the English fleet withdrew to Gibraltar. On 29 September a fleet of twenty-one men o'war sailed for Portsmouth, under Rear Admiral Sir Clowdisley Shovell. During the afternoon of 22 October, the fleet took soundings from which it was deduced they were at the mouth of the English Channel, but in fact were much further north than anticipated. The 3rd rate *Lenox,* 6th rate *Valeur,* and the fireship

Phoenix, captain Michael Sansom, were then despatched to Falmouth to escort a convoy, but as darkness fell found themselves amongst the Western Rocks of Scilly. The two larger men o'war escaped and anchored in St. Mary's Road, but the *Phoenix* struck Smith's Rock in Broad Sound, and only just managed to reach Tresco Sound, where she sank near New Grimsby harbour, remaining there for almost three months undergoing repair.

The main fleet continued on an easterly course, the weather thick and stormy, until at about 8 p.m. the *Association,* captain Edward Loades, which was in the van, struck the Outer Gilstone, SE of the Bishop Rock and sank with all hands. The *St. George* also struck but was lifted clear of the rocks by a large wave and survived, the *Eagle,* captain Robert Hancock being lost on Tearing Ledge, and the *Romney,* captain William Coney, somewhere close at hand. The fireship *Firebrand,* captain Francis

14

Piercey, struck in the vicinity but managed to stagger east along the southern edge of the Western Rocks, where she turned into the Sound between the islands of St. Agnes and Annet, struck the Menglow rock and sank, only a short distance from the St. Agnes lighthouse. The total number of officers and men on board the four lost ships is uncertain, but it has been estimated that some 1,400 lives were lost, the second worst disaster in the history of the Royal Navy, the first being the Great Storm of 1703. Only a quartermaster, named George Lawrence, said to be a butcher by trade, from Hull, survived out of the three larger ships. The *Firebrand's* captain, 1st Lieutenant, boatswain, carpenter, surgeon and fifteen men and boys also escaped.

The bodies of Sir Clowdisley Shovell, Edmund Loades, Sir John Narborough and James Narborough(the admiral's step-sons), Bishop Trelawney's son and the admiral's pet greyhound said to be named Mumper, are said to have been washed ashore in Porth Hellick, where the former was buried just above the high tide line. His corpse was said to have been found by a woman who robbed it of a valuable emerald ring, another version stating that she murdered him, and only confessed to this on her death bed. This suggests that the admiral and his associates managed to get away in a barge, but most contemporary accounts were based on hearsay and it is possible that it was not the stern of the barge that drifted into Porth Hellick, but the complete stern board of the *Association,* bearing an elaborate carved coat of arms which now hangs on the wall of the Magistrates' Court at Penzance.

The body of Sir Clowdisley Shovell was dug up a few days later, taken on board the man o'war *Salisbury,* conveyed to the Citadel at Plymouth where it was embalmed, and from there to a state funeral in Westminster Abbey. An extract from the *London Letter* of 9 July 1710, a Scottish newspaper reported:

'We hear from Scilly that the gentlemen concerned in the wreck where Sir Clowdisley Shovell was cast away have taken (from the bottom) several iron guns and seven brass guns, with a cable, and have found the *Association* in four fathom at low water, the hull of the ship being whole, wherein there is a vast treasure . . . the Queen's Plate, several chests of money, besides ten chests of Sir Clowdisley's own, with great riches of the Grandees of Spain. The divers go down in a copper engine, and continue two hours underwater, 30 fathoms deep, where they have also met with the Fireship, (cast away at the same time as the *Association,* I don't know her name. Had not the winds been westerly, which occasioned the seas to be very high and boisterous, all the treasure before this, had been fished out)'.

The wrecks of the *Association, Eagle* and *Firebrand* have all been located and heavily salvaged, the remains of the former having been located by Royal Navy divers in 1967 after a three year search.

1720 - A Dutch vessel was lost with all hands on Great Wingletang. December - *Mary,* of Nevis, was lost with her master and three crew.

1721 - 5 February. The brigantine *Hester,* master Marshall, from Carolina, was wrecked but the crew saved.

1730 - A ship, master Roberts, from the Canary Islands with wine, was lost on the island of Rosevear. Local fishermen went to her assistance saving some of the crew, but her master refused to leave on account of having a large sum of money on board. The weather became worse, and he and another man got ashore on the island where they lashed themselves to a rock. They remained there three whole days before being rescued. Many of the crew were lost.

1733 - A ship from the Bay of Honduras to London with mahogany logwood, was lost on the island of Melledgan. Her master and one man were found by a St. Agnes boat two days later, floating on a raft.

1736 - The *Flying Fish,* of Jamaica was wrecked. 9 October - *Triumph,* master William Cross, Jamaica to London with sugar, cotton, indigo, wood and other valuable goods, was wrecked near the Steval in a violent gale. The master, carpenter, boatswain and several seamen jumped overboard and drowned, but the surgeon, mate and a few seamen who remained on board the wreck were saved, some being thrown ashore on the round-house when she broke up, others on floating wreckage. Some were lost in an attempt to save the £10,000 worth of gold said to be on board, others managing to bring some of the bags of gold dust ashore.

'The Captain (being sensible of his inevitable Fate) recommended the Money to the Care of the Living, being about 10,000 £. Specie. The rich Furniture was saved by the islanders, as Part of the Cargo, with a considerable Quantity of the Money, which was divided among the Salvors, though the then *Commanding Officer* took proper Share of it into Possession for the Widow of the deceased Master. This Accident was said to be owing to the ill Conduct of the *Crew* intoxicating themselves with *Rum,* at coming into the Soundings, and the thick Weather, by the Account of those who escaped.' (Edward Heath, see p6).

1737 – A Dutch ship ran ashore in Wingletang Bay during a south-easterly gale. The master and one man were drowned.
April – An unidentified vessel, master Stut, Bristol to Falmouth with groceries, went ashore in Old Grimsby harbour. Crew saved. Her cargo was saved, put into cellars and re-shipped.
November – ***Betsy,*** of Bideford, master Hogg, from Malaga to Amsterdam with raisins and Barbary goat skins, foundered off Scilly.
All lost except for the master and two men who saved themselves in the ship's boat.
Endeavour – wrecked (the year may have been 1738).

1738 – 28 April. An unidentified vessel belonging to Gt.Yarmouth,   for Havre de Grace with wheat, master William Nicholls, was lost in Porthcressa on a rock later named after him. The crew were saved, as was some of the cargo, although in a damaged state.
November – ***Diana,*** of Calais, laden with wool, drove ashore on Mincarlo and was lost with all hands. Only a small part of the cargo was saved.

1739 – ***Griffin,*** of Gt.Yarmouth, from Scilly to Le Havre with wheat, drove ashore and became a total wreck.
William & Elizabeth, of London, was wrecked, but much of her cargo was recovered (the year may have been 1740).

30 December. **Mermaid,** of Plymouth, master Nicholas Mitchell, homeward bound from Bristol, drove ashore on Crow Bar. The crew were saved, but the ship lost.

30 December – **St. Joseph,** of Dunkirk, master James Billard, homeward bound from Schiedam, was lost near Samson. Sixty 'pieces' of brandy cargo were saved. 'The natives carried off ten pieces(barrels) and when the officers went to Samson the natives took them to Tresco. Officers and men from the man o'war **Duke of Cornwall** landed on Tresco, found the brandy and put it under lock and key, but then the locals broke into the warehouse and took it back.

1740 – **Diligence,** of Liverpool, from hence to Rotterdam with brandy, drove ashore and became a total wreck.

Baltic, of about 300-tons, was taken by a Spanish privateer.

1 January – **Jane,** master Thomas Barry, from Newfoundland to London with a cargo of grain, oil and fish, went ashore.

1 January – **Hannah,** of London, master Archibald Tiddall, from Lisbon with salt, went ashore and was wrecked. Crew saved.

19 August – 'Advice came yesterday of a Ship, the name unknown, being lost off Scilly. she is supposed from Maryland.'

1741 – **Marigold,** of Clovelly, for Falmouth, with a general cargo, was lost.

Susanna, of Appledore, for Rotterdam with butter, was wrecked.

1742 – **Margaret & Sarah,** carrying a general cargo, was wrecked.

9 March – **Nancy,** master William Walker, London to Dublin with compound spirits, hemp, iron, gunpowder and other merchandise, caught fire in New Grimsby harbour and blew up, causing the earth to shake and breaking several windows. Only a boy was on board at the time, asleep below, who was killed. It was supposed the ship's cat knocked a burning candle over on some hemp and set her on fire.

1743 – 11 January. Extract from a letter from Lieut. Thomas Hutchinson, of his Majesty's ship **Argyle,** to Captain Harrison of the said ship dated on board the **Convener,** tender at Scilly: 17.12.1742. 'I found riding here two West Indiamen; as soon as it was moderate, and got our Ship in a safe Road, I waited on the Governor according to my Instructions, he told me he would assist me in anything on his Majesty's Service; from him I waited on Captain Ellis, Commander of the **Richmond,** one of the West Indiamen and informed him I was in his Majesty's ship **Argyle's** Tender, and that I was obliged to press his Hands from him; he told me he would deal upon Honour with me, and would give me a list of his People. I then asked him if he thought I should meet any Difficulty in taking them, he told me no, for that he had wrote to his Mate to secure the Arms Chest, and that I should be received in quite a different manner than what I afterwards was. We mann'd both Boats in order to go on board them; but when we came near the Ship they told us to keep off, they would not suffer us to come on board; on which I immediately returned and weighed the Tender, and stood close under their Stern, and capitulated with them, telling them I was impressing for his Majesty's ship **Argyle,** if they would come voluntarily with me for her they should meet with a kind Reception. Otherwise I must be obliged to board them; their Answer was, so I might if I would; upon that I boarded them on the Starboard Quarter, Mr Northcot and several Men enter'd them. The Ship dropping astern, we let go the Anchor and immediately manned the Boats, and went in one of them myself, but found they had retir'd to close Quarters, and fir'd several Muskets at our People, from which they kill'd John Whitton, and wounded John Evans, since dead, and wounded Henry Dunn in the Leg, that he is since dead. But when I found they had retired to close Quarters I immediately turned all the rest of the People into the Boat, and went on board with them. The bloody Villains fir'd at us after we were put off; but, as God would have it, miss'd every Body. We took one of the Villains on board their own Ship, who had presented a Musket to Mr Northcot's breast, and certainly would have kill'd him, had not one of our Men knock'd him down; so shall take care of him for an Example. They have since Hailed the Ship for a Boat, and I have now got about one or two and twenty of them on Board. The Ship is in a very bad Condition, and the Captain tells me he must be obliged to put into Plymouth to repair her, so he is determined on it, and has wrote his owners Word so.' **Nancy,** master

Thomas Marshall, Londonderry to London with linen cloth, struck Green Island and was obliged to discharge some of her cargo. Of eighty-three packs discharged, only fourteen arrived at the St.Mary's warehouse!

Catherine, carrying a general cargo, caught fire and became a wreck.

Maria Adriana, master Jan Elswout, a Dutch East Indiaman, homeward bound from Batavia to Zeeland, is said to have foundered one mile off the Bishop Rock, whilst carrying 250,000 gold ducats(valued at several million pounds today), but research in VOC. (Verenigde Oostindische Compagnie –Dutch East India Company) records at the Hague show she disappeared with all hands, believed to be about 90 crew and passengers, somewhere between the Cape of Good Hope and Patria. Her cargo was valued at only 141,243 guilders, and there is no mention of her carrying gold.

Unidentified, a Dutch vessel was lost on Merrick Island, between Gweal and Heathy Hill, Bryher. Her crew saved themselves by felling a mast and scrambling over it to reach the island.

14 June – By letters from St. Mary's; 'We have Advice that a vessel laden with corn, master Briton, sprung a Leake off that place and was lost with all her Cargo, but the Men save'd themselves in their boat.'

13 July - *Hollandia,* master Jan Kelder, a Dutch East Indiaman of 1,150 tons, on her maiden voyage from Amsterdam to Batavia carrying silver specie and a general cargo, with 276 passengers, crew and soldiers, struck the Gunners and sank west of George Peters Ledge, off Annet, with all hands. The wreck lay undiscovered until 1971 when its silver specie treasure was recovered, along with bronze cannon and a great many artifacts.

1744 – 26 June. 'The *Kennington* Man of War has brought into Scilly a large French Ship which was taken some Time ago by the *Kennington* and the *Augusta,* suppos'd to be a French Man of War, but prov'd a West India Ship, and is said to be worth £9,000, the *Augusta* being one of the Convoy for the Newfoundland Fleet, sail'd with the Ships from thence for that Place.'

'The Prize taken by the *Kinsale* Man of War, Capt. Young, and sent into Scilly, proved to be a large ship from Martinico valued at £80,000.'

3 July – Extract from a Letter from Scilly dated June 17th:- 'The *St. Pier* bound from St. Domingo in Hispaniola, the prize lately taken by the *Kinsale* Man of War, is here, valued at £80,000. Six Sail of French merchant ships, bound from the West Indies, were also taken, and carrying to Newfoundland by the said Man of War, but a Storm arising, some of them parted at Sea, and it is thought two Sail of the French men with English Hands on Board are sail'd for London. The *Fame* is here, also the *Wager,* from Jamaica to London, and a snow, Master Curling, from Santa Cruz.'

28 June – The *Phoenix* Man of War is order'd to Scilly to Convoy the *Martinico Man,* the *Kinsale's* Prize, and several other Vessels that wait there for Convoy.

10 July – 'Yesterday came into St. Helen's Road the *St. Pierre,* Prize, taken 14th May 93 Leagues West of Scilly, Burthen 500 tons, loaded with Sugar, Coffee and Cotton; taken by the *Kinsale.'*

1745 – *Phoenix,* from South Carolina with rice, was taken by a French Privateer near Scilly and a prize crew put on board. However, she got amongst the rocks and was conducted by local fishermen into St. Mary's Road under the guns of the Garrison. The four fishermen and a boy involved subsequently received £3,000 salvage money (a huge sum of money in those days) from London merchants. The *Phoenix* sailed in convoy for the Isle of Wight, but was wrecked on the Wolf Rock. With the exception of two Scillonians (probably pilots), her crew were all saved.

19 September. *Draper,* of Rotterdam, master Baffner, from Rotterdam for Dublin with brandy, wine and a general cargo, was lost. The greater part of her cargo was saved.

1748 – *Thelma,* with saltpetre, was lost. The *Phoenix,* with iron bars was also lost.

24 February. *Sea Flower,* of Whitehaven, master Robert Curry, from Whitehaven for Rotterdam with 189 hogsheads of tobacco, was wrecked. Only 14 hogsheads were saved, the balance being so damaged as to be useless.

27 February. *Lizard,* HM sloop of war, 10-14 guns, 272 tons, Captain

Sission, was lost with all hands, about 110, on the Seven Stones. Another vessel was wrecked on Pednathise Head.

2 November. 'The ***Berwick,*** master Traile, from Barbados to London, who was taken on the 11th Instant off Scilly, is since re-taken by the ***Thetis*** man o'war, and sent into Plymouth.'

1748-9 – May. ***Two Sisters,*** for Dublin, put into Scilly leaky.

1750 – A large vessel struck on Pednathise Head and was lost with all hands.

March. ***Sumaton,*** master Gibson, from Oporto for North Yarmouth, 'riding under Scilly in a strong Gale of Wind, with all her Anchors and Cables out, was oblig'd to cut away and leave them.'

1751 – 20 April. ***Johanna***, Topsham to Swansea, master Whiteway, wrecked on Little Smith, St.Agnes.

1752 – A Dutch vessel, from Smyrna with cotton, was lost on Rosevear, but all hands were saved.

1753 – 15 November. ***Britannia***, ' – on Thursday last, Captain George Davis, bound to Philadelphia, was lost on the Woolpack, and the ship and cargo except two anchors which were saved by the assistance of boats, as were some of the passengers. The people drowned on board the ship are the Commander, George Davis; James Davis, son of the Commander, a youth of about 15 years of age; William Currie; Michael Dongean & John Leave, seamen. Mrs Leave, the wife of John Leave, who died in her husband's arms; four Dutch women and three Dutchmen, so that thirteen were drowned out of twenty-six. The cargo was worth upwards of £20,000.'

1754 – 6 December. ***Granville,*** master Knox, from Boston for London, went ashore at Scilly. Most of the cargo was saved, 'and 'tis thought the Ship will be got off.'

1755 – 25 April. *Neptune*, master Everets, a vessel from Smyrna for Rotterdam with general cargo, animal hair, silk and cotton was lost. Part of the cargo was salved.

29 August. *Providence*, Madeira to London, master Brown, lost.

1756 – 30 April. *Industry*, Malaga to Plymouth was lost with a boy and a female passenger drowned.

December. *Happy Jennet,* master Stewart (or Stuart), from Falmouth to Naples carrying fish, was lost off Scilly, but the crew we saved.

1757 - Letter from Scilly dated 11 January, St.Mary's, '- the *Hunter*, cutter, Richard Westcott Cdr. having on 31st ult. brought into this harbour a large French vessel from St. Domingo, and being by contrary winds under necessity of lying at anchor here; on the 5th day of this instant, was requested to weigh anchor and give Chase to a small Vessel hovering on this Coast, the same being suspected to be a Smuggler, and French Privateer, or a Spy on these Islands, or on the Trading Vessels in these Harbours; which he readily and cheerfully complied with, and gave chase to, and took her. It proved to be a small Sloop from Guernsey, with prohibited Goods, which on the 7th were secured in his Majesty's Customs at St.Mary's. It is hoped that the Readiness which Mr Westcott showed on this Occasion will recommend him to the Notice of those who have it in their Power to Reward the Brave, which is sincerely wished, by, Your Constant Reader . . . Republicus.'

April. *Craven,* master Stewart, from Jamaica for London, foundered whilst leaving St. Mary's.

27 July. *Elizabeth,* master Robertson, from Oporto for Hull, is lost on the Seven Stones.

1758 – 20 January. *Furnace,* of London, master William Park, for Gosport with brandy, oil, prunes, resin and pewter, was wrecked on Broad Ledge after striking Guthers Island. Most of her cargo was saved.

26 January. *Friendship,* from London to Bristol with wheat and flour etc. was wrecked, vessel and cargo lost.

9 April. 'By our Correspondent at Penzance we are informed that on

The Liverpool registered iron barque *Maipu,* carrying a cargo of saltpetre, was wrecked in fog on the rocks in Hell Bay, Bryher, 27 July 1879, whilst on passage from Iquique to Hamburg.

Acknowledgment: Frank Gibson

Thursday 9th instant, a Sloop of Lynn bound to Liverpool with Wheat and Barley, was taken between the Land's End and Isles of Scilly by the **Bellona** Privateer of St. Malo, mounting 20 Carriage Guns and full of Men, who ransomed her for 100 Guineas. On 19th Instant the said Privateer was cruizing off the Isles of Scilly to intercept the Coasting trade, and there were then between 70 and 80 Sail there.'

12 May. 'Notice is hereby given that a Survey will be held on Friday the 12th day of May next ensuing, at 2 o'clock in the Afternoon, at the House of Mr William Cock at the Island of St. Mary's in Scilly, for selling about 1,500 Gallons of French Prize Brandy, free of Duty for the payment of Salvage, pursuant to the Order of the Honourable Commissioners of his Majesty's Customs – also about 1,800 gallons of Brandy for exportation. At the same time and place will also be sold in several Lots, the following Goods, viz:- French Prize Goods – 135 chests and a Half of Sallad Oyl; 1 Cask of Rosin; 37 Barrels of Porter; seven Bags of Hops.

Samples of the above Brandy and Oyl may be seen and tasted any time before the Day of Sale at the House of Mr John Batten, Merchant, in Penzance.'

25 October. **Gracia Devina,** of Venice, from Cadiz for London with cochineal and silks, was lost with some of her crew. 11 December. Notice. 'Whereas the Ship **Gracia Devina** Captain Petriua, laden with valuable goods was lately wrecked on Scilly, and whereas there is Reason to believe that a great Part of the Cochineal and Silks have the same been offered for sale at Penzance and in that Neighbour-hood, the Proprietors of the said cargo have thought it proper to give this Publick notice to all Persons who have saved part of the cargo, that they are desired to bring the same to the King's Ware-house at Scilly . . . but if any part of the said Cargo shall hereafter be discovered to have been saved and sold, or like-wise concealed, the Persons concerned will be prosecuted as the Law dictates.'

20 November. An account says that the **Gratia Devina** struck on a sunk Rock some Distance from the Island; 29 Men escaped in the Long Boat, 50 Men were left on Board who perished. The Ship was immediately beat in Pieces and little or nothing saved. Her Cargo consisted of 350 Butts of Currants, 64 Bales of Silk, 70 Bags of Cochineal and betwixt 30 and

40,000 Pounds Sterling in Dollars (ie. approximately 160,000 silver dollars)'.

2 November. *Venetian*, Coding to London was wrecked.

December. *Hampton,* master Pearson, from Whitehaven for Southampton, was lost. The crew and part of the cargo were saved.

22 December. *Scipio,* master Watson, from Jamaica for London with rum, was lost with all hands. Two puncheons of rum were saved.

1759 – 28 February. *Fortune*, master Neskill, Genoa to London, carrying oranges and lemons, was stranded and lost.

12 March. *Pretty Peggy*, master Nashall, Ancona to London, lost.

16 October. *Pownall*, master James Caloe, Boston to London:
'Admiralty Office, November 12th. Pursuant to an act of Parliament passed into the 20th year of his Majesty's reign, this is to give notice to those concerned that information hath been sent to this office from the Collector of His Majesty's Customs at Scilly, that the snow *Pownall*, laden with whale oil, sugar, tar, turpentine and staves, was lost the 16th inst. of the last month on Crebbaweden(sic), one of the Scilly Islands; and that some part of her cargo and the eight crew were saved.'

October. *Speedwell,* of London, from Jamaica for London with rum and sugar, was lost on the Seven Stones. The crew were saved. A Snow, 120 tons, from Boston for London with spermaceti, was lost.

1760 – A Dutch vessel with wine and paper, was lost on the Biggal of Melledgan, with two of her crew. The remainder got ashore on an island where they were found the next morning.

30 June. The *Eagle,* frigate, Captain Knill, bound from Bristol for London, has taken a French Privateer of one Gun and four Swivels off Scilly, and carried her in there, and sold her for sixty Guineas.

October. *Nostra Senora de Muriel,* a Spanish vessel, master Martin Supena, from Bilbao for the Isle of Man was lost, but the crew saved.

1762 – A French vessel was lost on Rosevean. Six men managed to reach the island on pieces of wood, but twelve were drowned.

April. *Katherine,* master Bolton, from South Carolina to Bristol, was taken to the Westward of Scilly, by a Bayonne privateer of 16 guns.

1763 – March. *Europa,* master Stevens, from London to Lisbon with corn, foundered, but the crew were saved.

July. *Gallaway,* master Smith, from St. Kitts to London, was lost on the Seven Stones Reef. A woman and a Negro were saved.

1764 – A Dutch galliot, from Bordeaux to Hamburg with wine, struck on the Lethegus Rock and became a total loss.

A vessel laden with coal for St. Agnes lighthouse was lost on Burnt Island, but all hands were saved.

A Portuguese vessel, with a cargo of wine, was lost with all hands on the Brow of the Ponds (another account gives a date of 1784).

17 February. *Duke of Cumberland,* master Duputron, with pilchards, was lost, but her cargo saved.

April. *Venus,* master Robertson, from New York to Newry, with linseed, was towed in bottom up. There was no trace of her crew.

November/December. *Eagle,* master Bilby, from Peterborough to Bristol, was lost at Scilly.

1765 – April. *Charleston,* master Mills, from South Carolina to London with rice, stranded and became a total loss, 150 barrels of cargo was saved.

May. A Dutch vessel from Bayonne to Bremen with wine, stranded and became a total wreck.

1766 – January. The following ships, bound for London, put into Scilly by 'contrary winds, viz. the *Pitt, Ross* and the *Bella,* master Barrass, from Jamaica; and the *Pellegrine,* master Flynn, from Leghorn.

December. A French vessel, with pilchards, was lost at Scilly, the crew saving themselves in their own boat.

11 December. *Expedition,* master Smith, from Liverpool to London, stranded amongst the islands, crew saved.

19 December. *Seahorse*, master James, carrying pilchards from Zand(sic) to London was wrecked. Crew saved in their own boat.

1767 – A small vessel foundered half a mile from the shore at Porth Minnick. Only one man was saved.

December. *Mercury,* master Foss, took fire alongside the quay and burnt out.

1768 – May. *Alexander,* master Cobb, foundered in the approaches to Scilly on passage from Lisbon to London.
8 August. *Duchess of Leinster*, Dublin to Dunkirk in ballast, master Sinnot, 'foundered 3 leagues off Cape Cornwall. The crew took to their boat and next day got in to St.Mary's Pier, Scilly.'

1769 – January. *Sally,* master William Living, was at anchor in Porthcressa when lost.
October. *John & Ann,* master Wareham, from Dublin to London, was wrecked, but her crew and cargo were saved.
November. *Brothers,* master May, from Bideford to Falmouth, was lost off the islands.

1771 – A vessel with a cargo of salt was lost at Porth Loggos. One of her anchors was found later on Salakee Down, covered with stones. An unidentified vessel was lost with all hands on Cuckold's Ledge, near the Gugh, St. Agnes.
21 January. *Joseph & Betsey,* master Thomas Forewood, was lost on a sunken rock coming out of Scilly, due to the fault of a St. Mary's pilot.
30 January. *Joseph & Betty,* Lieut. Isaac Vailant, RN. a hired Royal Navy press-gang tender, on passage from Fowey to Glasgow, foundered off Scilly, her crew reaching the islands.
5 March. *Petworth,* master Ford, was lost on the 5th instant on a rock off St. Martin's, part of her cargo was saved but damaged.
October. *Douglas,* master Brackanridge, from the Mosquito Shore to England, foundered offshore.
November. *London,* master Walker, a packet vessel, Bordeaux to London, was lost at Scilly.

1772 – January. *Margaret Thrasher,* master Thrasher, Newfoundland to Poole, split in two on striking the rocks, her crew all lost but for two men who stayed on the rock for three days before being rescued.

1773 – *Felicity,* master Nichollas Langolis, from St. Domingo to Le Havre, with indigo, coffee, sugar and cotton, ran ashore on St. Mary's. Ship and cargo were lost, together with her master, mate and other crew members, but her 2nd mate seven sailors and a Negro female were saved.

25 September. *Duke of Cumberland,* master Seth Paddock, of Boston, Mass., to London with oil, deals, timber and lumber, was lost on St. Helen's. Most of the cargo was lost but the crew saved.

8 October. *John & Mary* master Duff, of Scilly, drove on the rocks of St. Martin's and after receiving considerable damage, was taken to St. Mary's. The cargo received much damage.

16 December. *Squirrel,* master French, from Lisbon to Dublin, was wrecked off St. Martin's.

1774 – February. *Molly,* master Boroudale, from London to Liverpool was lost on the Seven Stones.

16-17 October. A Dutch galliot, of 120 tons, carrying salt, 'was taken up on the stream, dismasted, about ten Leagues from these islands, without a living creature on board. She was towed into Scilly where the Collector put the salt into warehouses for the security of the duty and benefit of the proprietors that should appear to claim it, and also for the just salvors, in doing which he was obliged to call the Military for assistance to quell the rioters, and in their presence to read the Riot Act. Several people declared positively that the Collector was obliged to leave the salt in the vessel and to protest against their illegal proceedings. The mob afterwards dispersed, and the salt, about 15,000 bushels, 84lbs each, was cellared.'

December. *Elizabeth Line,* Cadiz to Dartmouth, was lost in Scilly.

1775 – January. *Nimrod,* master Ash, foundered in Scilly.

February. *Weddel,* master Francis Thorp, carrying cloth and iron, stranded on a rock amongst the islands near Old Grimsby, and beached at Hugh Town being rendered incapable of sailing having received so much damage.

December. A large Dutch ship with sugar, coffee etc., name unknown, was lost off Scilly and eighteen of her people drowned.

1776 – 6 February. *Thomas,* master Wilhelm Rhode, a galliot, carrying coffee, indigo, sugar and wine from Bordeaux to Hamburg was lost on St. Mary's. For robbing the cellar in which a small portion of her salvaged cargo was stored, a Custom House boatman from Scilly was transported for seven years.

February. *Triumph,* master Fletcher, parted her cable in a gale and stranded on a rock at Scilly, and both ship and cargo were lost.

Lyon, master Boyman, from Boston, Mass., to Portsmouth with baggage and several wounded soldiers, was wrecked at Scilly, the *John,* master Hunter, taking the goods and soldiers on to Portsmouth.

May. *Duke of Cumberland,* Virginia to Falmouth foundered off Scilly, only one man saved.

1777 - 24 February. *Hunter,* master John Kennedy, a brig from Lisbon to London carrying wine, oil and fruit, was wrecked on St. Mary's and broken up.

15 April. *Three Sisters,* of Rigwald, Pomerania, master John Cruse, from Liverpool to the Baltic with salt, ran on some rocks and was lost. Her master and crew, ten in total, saved themselves in their own boat.

May. *Joseph* master Ottero, Bilbao to Exeter, with nuts and iron, was lost at Scilly, and all the crew perished.

August. *Margaret & Mary,* master Izat, from Halifax to London, was taken the 28th ult. by the *Mars,* privateer of 22 guns, off Scilly.

6 August. Captain's log of HMS *Foudroyant.* 'Moderate and fine clear weather; at 2 stood off and on towards St. Mary's for a boat to come off to gain intelligence. At 4 the Collector of Customs came on board, at 7 stood off under easy sail, the lighthouse on St. Agnes N by E. 3 or 4 miles.'

4 December. A transport vessel from Boston, Mass., for Portsmouth, with wounded soldiers, was driven ashore on the west side of Taylor's Island, having dragged her anchors in the Roads. All on board were saved, but the vessel became a total loss.

4 December. Wreckage from a vessel, presumed to be Venetian from the colours cast up on St. Mary's. A few currants were salvaged from her cargo.

1779 – 27 January. 'This day was brought in two French privateers, taken off Scilly by a privateer belonging to Liverpool, after a short engagement.'

7 April. *Tartar,* privateer of Penzance, foundered 6 leagues off Scilly. The crew were taken up by a fishing boat, and carried to Penzance.

October. *Theris*, a prize to the *Swallow* of Jersey, foundered west-south-west of Scilly.

9 December. *Friendship,* master Francis Blecker, of Amsterdam, homeward bound from St. Eustatia with tobacco, sugar, coffee, cocoa and indigo, became a total loss. All the crew were saved.

1780 – January. A vessel said to be a French 36-gun frigate, was lost with all hands on Pednathise Head.

17 January. *Christian,* master Andreas Becher, a snow from Liverpool to Ostend with pepper, coffee, hides and other goods, was obliged to cut her cables and run ashore. A sale of her cargo took place on St.Mary's in June the following year.

16 January. *Pheasant,* master John Rawlinson, from Newfoundland and Ireland with codfish, beef, port and butter, was driven ashore. The vessel was lost but part of the cargo saved.

16 January. *Glory* master Moses Lewis, from Plymouth to Dublin with sugar, tobacco and wine, drove ashore.

8 February. A brig of Plymouth was lost at Scilly, and 'great damage has been done along the coast'.

31 August. *Tryal,* a Bristol brig, letter of marque, homeward bound from St. Christopher and Nevis with sugar and cotton, was wrecked in Crow Sound. Part of her cargo was saved.

November. *Charming Molly,* master Samuel Marder, a Weymouth brig of 120-tons for Dublin with Portland stone, stranded near Bryher and became a total loss.

30 December. *Maria Clara,* a French brig captured as a prize by a Jersey privateer, master John Messervy, with timber, was wrecked on the rocks near Carn Morval Point.

1781 – February. *Conquerant,* a French 3rd rate man o'war, 74 guns and 700 crew, one of three large French warships said to have been lost off the islands in the same night with all hands, which could total approximately 1,640 (more men than in the 1707 *Association* disaster). Whilst there are printed English sources that confirm the incident, standard reference works for ships of the French Navy exclude any vessel of this name for the period.

Julie, a French 5th rate man o'war, 44 guns, 340 crew. A French warship, possibly a frigate, lost at the same time as the other enemy vessels, which are believed to have been attempting a landing on Scilly with a view to capturing the islands at night.

Le Priarus, a French 3rd rate man o'war, 74 guns, 600 crew, lost during the same night as the previous two vessels, believed to have sunk in heavy weather south of St. Agnes.

31 March. *Endeavour*, a Teignmouth brig, master John Langdon, Liverpool to Portsmouth with rum, brandy, coal and herrings, was lost on St. Helen's. Part of the cargo saved, as were all the crew.

May. *Jason*, a Dunkirk privateer, master Patrick Callagan, drove on the rocks of SE Scilly and foundered. Of her 170 crew 80 were saved.

7 July. *St. Antonio de Lisboa*, master Jose Francisco le Nacimento, of 100 tons, Oporto to London with olive oil and wine, was lost in Scilly 'on the rocks'. Some of her cargo drove ashore, 'After it was saved, some of the inhabitants insisted on one half in kind, before they would carry any part to the warehouse, which the surveyor and officers of the Customs absolutely refused to comply with. They were persuaded so to do by Abraham Leggatt, surgeon of the Garrison, who insisted that the officers of the Customs had no right to interfere, as it was a dead wreck, so they took it by force. The Collector, upon receiving information of divers quantities of wine, part of the cargo, being secreted, applied to the Commanding Officer for a warrant to search, and in a suspected house on Tresco, found two hogsheads of wine secreted therein, which the master of the house denied him from carrying to the warehouse and swore he would knock out the Collector's brains with an iron poker which he had in his hand, before the wine be removed to the King's warehouse.'

1782 – *Maria Charlotta*, belonging to Johann Schmidt, of Prussia, about 200 tons, was found dismasted on the strand about half a league off and brought into Brhyer. She was deserted and no papers could be found. Her cargo was French wine, red and white, and vinegar. One half of the cargo was placed in the King's warehouse, the islanders, at the instigation of Mr Leggatt, the Garrison surgeon, detaining the other half as salvage. This gentleman 'had the audacity to present a pistol to an officer in the execution of his duty in taking down advertisements put up to stimulate the islanders in their illegal proceedings.' The legal percentage of salvage was one third.

New York, a brig, master William Baker, 100 tons, London to Antigua with mail, Irish beef, pork and biscuits, was wrecked in Porthmellon.

2 February. *Lady Johanna,* master David Giston, Demerara to London, with coffee, sugar, cotton, cocoa and rum, drove ashore. The cargo was saved and the vessel sold and broken up.

14 July. *Madonna de Carmine,* master Bassele Vuccossaniach, a Venetian ship, Rotterdam to Smyrna with cloth, was lost on Golden Ball Bar. The crew saved themselves with great difficulty, together with their belongings and some of the cloth which, being greatly distressed, they sold to the islanders. They hired a small sloop in order to reach Falmouth.

13 August. *Providentia Divina,* master Pascal Halina, a Venetian ship, from Marseilles to London (and possibly Ostend) with Castile soap, wine, almonds and olive oil, struck on the Crim and broke up, drowning two of her crew. Some escaped on a raft made of wreckage. A boat, which put out to look for salvage, saw the raft with eleven men on it, so benumbed with cold that only two could stand. They were landed at St. Agnes, too weak to walk. Many were badly cut and bruised in getting to the raft, especially a passenger who was in his bunk when she struck and came on deck naked, having no time to put on clothes. The sea was so rough other local boats had passed by the raft, afraid to go alongside for fear of being stove in. Three men were blown into New Grimsby Harbour on a mast from the vessel.

1783 –24 January, the brig *Oldenburger*, 130 tons, master Hedstrum, from St.Vincent to Ostend with a general cargo, dragged her anchors in New Grimsby Harbour and was wrecked.

7 February. A large unidentified Dutch built vessel was seen on the rocks with only four men aboard. They managed to reach the rocks before she broke up and sank.

23 February. *Fredericus*, a large Swedish vessel, drove ashore but no boats could put out to her assistance. Eventually the crew launched their long boat, and as many as the boat could hold got safely ashore. The remainder were lost when she foundered.

Several vessels reported as being wrecked in gales.

4 March. At midnight, during a south-west gale, a transport vessel from New York came in at the back of Bryher, and got in such a position that no pilot could have extricated her. Miraculously, she managed to anchor and was saved. Her Captain stated that he had spoken with an East Indiaman that night and feared she must be somewhere amongst the islands, whereupon boats went out and found the *Nancy*, master David Robertson, 300 tons, from Jamaica to London with rum, sugar and fustick(a tropical wood yielding a yellow dye), was lost on the Brow of Hellweathers.

31 July. *Agnetta*, America to Denmark with oil and tobacco leaf went ashore, ' – all lost except for three men and a boy.'

5 September. *Nancy*, an East India Company Packet, master Robert Haldane, carrying mail, passengers and cargo, struck first on the outer Gilstone and then drove ashore on Rosevear. Her passengers included officers returning from India and a Mrs. Cargill, said to be a well known actress who, having made her fortune in the east, was bringing it home, mostly in cash. Captain Scott of Hartlepool, whose ship had stranded on St.Mary's, went out with his men in boats and brought back the bodies of Mrs Cargill and two others, who were buried on the island. Other bodies were too far gone with putrefaction to be removed. The mail was saved and sent on to London, also some muslin, clothing and a small quantity of money was saved by islanders.

 5 September. *Financier*, master John Lobec, from Charleston to London with rice, tobacco and indigo, was lost two miles from the St.Agnes light-house at 10pm, ' – a very small part of the cargo saved; also another vessel was lost at the same place.'

25 November. A 700 ton vessel laden with deals lost in St.Helen's Gap.

9 December. A vessel reported to be from Wyburg to Liverpool, master Sandland, was lost at Scilly, ' – part of the cargo is expected to be saved.'

1784 – Several vessels wrecked in January in gales and fog.

26 March. *Robert & Sally*, master Brown, London to Lancaster, lost 'near Scilly.'

31 December. *Aurora*, master Dixon, carrying coal from Liverpool to London, struck a rock off Land's End, reached Scilly but sank in St.Helen's Gap. After her cargo was thrown overboard she was refloated and saved.

1785 – 7 January. *Phoenix*, master Gilbert Chrystie, registered at Amsterdam, on passage to Philadelphia, drove ashore at 4pm. 'A large Dutch ship deeply laden, with jury masts and very leaky, drove ashore and it is feared will go to pieces. Several vessels were sent to assist in saving the cargo.' On 21 February there was offered for sale by public auction on St.Mary's, ' – for exportation at the above place on Monday 10th March next, and on the following day, for cash or bank notes, the cargo of the schooner *Phoenix* lately stranded here, consisting of different merchandise viz: cordage, mercury, haberdashery, stationery, drapery, hats, steel, looking glasses, hardware etc. with a variety of other articles too tedious to be inserted here. The same to be viewed three days previous to the sale, at the stores of Mr Thomas Philips, Steward at Scilly, where attendance will be given by Messrs. Levy and Marcus.'

September. An unidentified vessel was wrecked.

November. *Expedition*, master Collins, of Dublin, drove ashore   and went to pieces. Her crew were on the rocks several hours before being rescued and taken to St.Mary's by a French vessel.

17 December. *Amiable Sarah*, of Dunkirk, master Cardier, from Port-au-Prince with sugar, coffee and indigo, was brought into Scilly by fishermen from Sennen, Cornwall. She had been found abandoned six miles off Land's End. Attempts had been made to scuttle her by boring holes in the cabin floor, cutting the rigging and lashing the pump gear. Surprisingly, 50 chests of silver dollars were found amongst the cargo.

1786 – 6 January. A large Dutch vessel drove ashore and was lost with all hands.

5 March. *Elizabeth*, a British vessel was lost amongst the Western Rocks.

'- Mr Noble, Mr Alexander and two other gentlemen, who were passengers were alone saved. The crew took to the longboat but unfortunately all perished. The news is brought by one of the above gentlemen who is just arrived in town.'

14 September. The weather was described as being 'tempestuous beyond description.' Every vessel in the roadstead had to put to sea and most were dismasted. A large American vessel, to Amsterdam with tobacco, drove ashore and became a total loss.'

1787 – 6 February. *Janus,* from Dunkirk to Cape Francois, was lost. A West Indiaman was said to have been lost on the Seven Stones.

24 December. *Betsy*, master Williams, a Chester brig carrying lead and empty casks from Chester to London, was lost on Bartholomew Ledge. The *Dowson*, master Best, was also lost, her crew saved.

24 December. *Duke of Cornwall*, master Hoskin, a brigantine of Penzance carrying a general cargo from London to Falmouth, was blown past Land's End to Scilly, and went ashore on Bartholomew Ledge where, 'very little of the cargo was saved for the proprietors.'

It was reported from Falmouth on 2nd January 1788 that, 'Advice has been received here that a brig employed in trading from this port and Penzance to London, being one of the ship's commonly called tin-ships, was a few days since, in a violent gale of wind, driven past this port and wrecked on St.Agnes, one of the Scilly Isles. The ship and cargo are totally lost, but the Captain and crew saved.'

1788 – 21 January. *Mary*, master Hughes, Truro to Swansea, lost. 7 June. A vessel from Virginia with tobacco, struck and sank on Pednathise Head. Her crew were saved.

3 November. *Terwagout*, master Salisbury, said to be a man o'war sloop, having taken a prize valued at £2,000, gave chase to a brig of Jersey but ran aground on the rocks at Scilly where she was lost.

10 December. A local boat from St.Mary's to Tresco sank in the Sound, nine men drowned, all of whom left large families.

1789 – 13 January. *Biscayneer*, Newfoundland to Dartmouth, was lost in Scilly. *Nottingham,* master Brown, from Faro to Rotterdam, ran upon the rocks going into Scilly. Both vessel and cargo was damaged and had to unload to repair. The mate was drowned.

24 February. *London*, master Alexander Curling, 280 tons, Charleston to London with rice, indigo and tobacco leaf, was lost on the Western Rocks with 15 of her 16 man crew. The sole survivor, Joseph Tuttle, ship's carpenter, was washed up on a rock and remained there for over two days before rescue. About 3,000 dollars and £150 in gold coins were saved from amongst the rocks where she was wrecked, the remaining specie being lost along with her cargo.

24 March. *Ann*, master Grant, Newfoundland to Vigo was lost.

May. A large Prussian brig carrying wine, was 'lost on the rocks.'

1790 – April. *Stormont*, master Thompson, from Cette to Guernsey, was wrecked close to Scilly.

5 June*. Eagle*, master John Rosseter, from Charleston to Falmouth with rice, tobacco leaf and barrel staves, reported lost amongst the Western Rocks. Crew saved in their own boat. A Customs & Excise advertisement read: 'By Order of . . . on Tuesday the 4th day of October next by 2 o'clock in the afternoon will be sold by public auction at St.Mary's, one of the Islands of Scilly(duty free for payment of salvage), a quantity of rice, tobacco leaf and staves etc.'

18 June. *Elizabeth*, master Wilson, at about 9 a.m. the wreck of this American ship, from Alicante with rice, barrel staves, tobacco and salt, was seen coming up with the tide, her decks gone and masts and rigging hanging over the side. Island boats took her in tow but could not make any headway. She was seen for several days in this condition, after which she ran ashore and broke up on the islands.

6 December. 'The improvement lately made in the light upon St. Agnes, one of the islands of Scilly, is spoken of very highly by nautical men who have seen it, as very well calculated to answer the ends proposed; namely to give a stronger light, and to be distinguished from any other light in the Channel. The light makes a revolution once in a minute, and consequently shows itself like a brilliant star, or flash of lightening in every direction once in that period; a distinction that cannot be mistaken . . .'

1791 – 14 January. *Briton,* London to Georgia, master Coningham, foundered with the loss of five crew 12 leagues off Scilly.

23 February. *Mercury* Georgetown to London, registered at Boston, Captain Mealley, laden with tobacco and staves was lost on the Western Rocks. Her crew landed by boat on St. Agnes. Her cargo was lost but 1,353 ounces of cut silver were saved.

14 March. 'Betwix't the hours of 5 and 6, Mr John Badge, here to fore master of the *Queen*, last of his Majesty's ship *Atlas*, in passing from St.Mary's to the island of Tresco where he resided, was overset in a small Norway skiff, with an invalid of this Garrison who attended him, by a squall and both were drowned. Mr.Badge was a man very much respected, and will be greatly lamented, and his loss most severely felt by his widow and eight children; the soldier also left a widow and four children. Both bodies and the boat also were taken up the next day at low water – the mast was found standing.'

4 April. 'Yesterday eleven pilots belonging to St.Mary's put to sea to take charge of a number of coasters, all in one boat, and blowing hard from the east and a very heavy sea the boat filled, and all were drowned. One man named Jenkyn was picked up on some of the materials which he had lashed together, alive, but was so exhausted that he expired. Amongst those who perished were four brothers named Watts.'

5 September. 'Last night the Custom House boat with Mr Hall, the Surveyor, 5 boatmen and an assistant, rowed within a boat's length of a smuggling vessel . . although no violence was offered by the crew of the Custom's boat, the smugglers fired repeatedly, by which inhuman proceeding John Oliver and William Millet fell and expired, the former received a shot through the chest, the latter by two or more balls through the head and chest, and being so very near, his brains were scattered in considerable quantities in the boat. John Jane was desperately wounded, his right cheek being nearly carried away and little hopes are entertained of his recovery . . an inquest has been held, the jury determined wilful murder . . the smuggling boat got off.'

1792 – 24 January. Three brigs which had been sheltering in Old Grimsby were driven to sea at night in a gale and all were lost.

1793 – A small vessel, a French prize, laden with timber, was lost on the west point of Taylor's Island. Her master had lost a vessel on Carn Morval Point some 10 or 12 years previous.

18 March. 'Arrived at Plymouth the sloop *Lively* of Scilly, a smuggler laden with 92 ankers of spirits: she was captured and brought in by the *Ranger* cutter, Captain Lane.'

9 April. *Brothers,* Poole to Newfoundland was lost at Scilly.

1794 – March. *James,* master Bieters, Carnarvon to London, foundered off Scilly after being run down.

4 October. *Henrietta,* a cutter, carrying part of the cargo of the *Beckford,* from Saffee, 'performing quarantine at Scilly, was drove on shore at Scilly on the 4th instant, the skins are landed.'

1795 – 17 February. *Garnet*, master Lambton, Halifax to Quebec, was driven right across the Atlantic by gales and had been three months at sea when she was wrecked on Scilly.

27 February. *Monmouth*, master Blackburn, Jamaica to London, taken by the French as a prize, was retaken by the *London Packet,* only to be lost on the rocks at Scilly. Two men drowned.

Unity, master Grill, from Oporto to Liverpool and an unidentified sloop were taken by the French and sunk off Scilly.

2 June. *Recovery*, master Bowen, of Bristol, Savannah to Falmouth, ran on the rocks near St. Mary's and filled with water.

13 October. *Zeelilie*, master Kornelis Adriaasz, a Zeeland Dutch East Indiaman, from Batavia, 54 guns and 69 crew, after being taken by HMS *Sceptre* near St. Helena, then escorted to Shannon and sent on to London, was lost between Little and Great Crebawethan at night, with 24 English crew drowned. She was part of the very last convoy of VOC.(Verenigde Oostindische Compagnie – Dutch East India Company) ships homeward bound before the Dutch East India Company was liquidated, and the *Zeelilie* carried the largest shipment of Chinese porcelain and tea ever carried. Her porcelain cargo, originally some 240 tons, representing about 4 million individual pieces, now lies on the seabed broken into small shards.

19 October. Several casks of Carlisle soap were washed ashore on St. Mary's, believed to be from a Mediterranean vessel lost locally.

Mid October. *Margaret,* master Chisholm, Liverpool to Charleston, was lost on the Western Rocks.

10 November. *Hope,* master Slighton, Jamaica to London, was lost near St. Mary's.

1796 – January. A vessel, thought American, went on shore on the Western Rocks of Scilly. Seven people drowned in attempting to go to their assistance. The brig *Vine,* master Leane, Jersey to Virginia, and the Danish brig *Freden,* Majorca to London, were both lost on the Western Rocks.

1797 – 6 January. *Mercury*, master Bulley, Scilly to London, was lost on Scilly, part of the cargo saved.

Early January. The transport vessels *Albion*, master Johnson, Ipswich to Bristol, and the *Juno* master Clark, London to Africa and the West Indies, were lost. The wreck of the *Juno* was found by divers near Hard Lewis in 1970, the ship's bell being recovered. *Sisters,* master Parker, Falmouth to Lisbon, was taken by a privateer and burnt off the islands.

31 October. A Danish vessel from the West Indies, master Andreas Birke, went on shore at Scilly and became a wreck.

19 October. A local fishing vessel from Mounts Bay to St. Martins, was lost near the Seven Stones with all five men on board.

1798 – 10 December. HMS *Colossus,* captain George Murray. A 3rd rate man o'war from the Mediterranean and Lisbon to Portsmouth, dragged her anchors in a gale in St. Mary's Roads and went ashore on Southward Wells, just south of Samson at dusk, fell over on her beam ends and became a total loss. Of her 600 odd crew, only one life was lost. She carried part of Sir William Hamilton's second collection of valuable Etruscan pottery and vases, most of which was lost. In addition on board was a lead coffin containing the body of Admiral Lord Shuldam which was saved. The wreck site was located in 1974 by divers. Designated by the

Secretary of State as a Protected Wreck, many thousands of pottery shards were recovered and sent to the British Museum for cataloguing. The wreck has since lost its protection order.

10 December. A captured French 14 gun, privateer brig, struck a rock when entering one of the Sounds at night and was lost with all hands.

12 December. *Mary & Betsey,* a sloop of Cardigan, was lost after being abandoned by her crew.

1799 – 8 February. *Nancy,* master Bridekirk, Waterford to London, put into Scilly in distress and unable to navigate, became a wreck.

22 February. *Lark,* master Newport, Waterford to Portsmouth, was lost at Scilly. Cargo saved.

April. *Caroline*, master Ellis, St. Michael's to London foundered at Scilly, all the crew were saved.

1800 – 17 January. *William,* master Elliston, Martinique to London, a full-rigged ship registered in Spain, armed with 10 x 4pdr guns, went ashore at Scilly and was lost.

1801 – 13 January. *Melantho,* master Richard Hardie, London to the West Indies, registered at Whitby, drove ashore at Porthloo on St. Mary's. Her 23 year old captain drowned in trying to get from the ship's boat onto a rock. She was refloated, repaired at St. Mary's and offered for sale in April 1802. Her cargo consisted of linen and drapery, mercury, hosiery, ironmongery, haberdashery, cutlery etc.

30 January. *Thomas & William,* master Jenkins, a sloop from Neath to Falmouth, was lost at Scilly.

2 November. *Esperance,* master William Barber, a brig carrying pilchards from Penzance to Venice, parted her cables at 10 a.m. in a gale in St. Mary's Roads and drove ashore on a reef between St. Mary's and Tresco. 'The crew remained on board in a very perilous situation for upwards of a hour, when, finding the vessel was falling to pieces, and no hope of assistance from the inhabitants, they at length ventured in their own boats, and happily reached the island of St. Martins in safety.'

9 December. *Sisters,* master John Wise, a brig from Newfoundland to Poole with whale oil, parted her cables at 5 a.m. in a gale and drove ashore to be lost on St. Mary's. Two crew drowned.

1802 – The brig *Francisco*, from Majorca for London, was lost on the Western Rocks.

13 February. *Fortune* a brig of Banff, London to Dublin with a general cargo, struck the Seven Stones and was abandoned. Four Scilly pilots boarded the derelict in an attempt to save her, but she sank suddenly and two of them drowned.

13 May. *Triton*, master Powell, Boston to Liverpool, foundered 10 leagues west of the islands, and her captain, mate and four seamen drowned, having lost her boats some days before in a gale. Three men clung to a grating until picked up by a fishing boat and landed on Scilly.

1803 – 25 January. *Caroline,* master Jennings, Limerick to Poole, was lost at Scilly, but the crew all saved.

Late May. *La Calipso,* master Scallier, and the *Freres,* master Colembemar, from Santo Domingo to Le Havre, were taken by the Revenue lugger *Providence* and taken into Scilly. *La Calipso* went ashore and became a total loss.

1 November. *Loyalty,* master Williams, Liverpool to Plymouth, drove ashore during the morning and both vessel and cargo lost.

18 November. Seven local men drowned whilst attempting to board a Batavian ship which appeared off the islands in distress. She was later taken by a small privateer cutter of Polperro and taken into St. Ives. Her cargo was said to have cost £90,000 in Batavia.

1804 – 30 May. *Quicksilver,* master Rolestone, a French full-rigged ship, carrying salt from London to Labrador, struck on Crow Bar and filled. The cargo was lost but the crew saved.

24 December. *Active,* master T. Morgan, 300 tons gross, a full-rigged ship, Portsmouth to Chepstow in ballast, was lost during an easterly gale, ' – the crew being saved by the exertions of our pilots'.

24 December. *Padstow,* master Stephens, carrying iron from Cardiff to London was lost on Scilly, all the crew and some of the cargo saved.

1805 – Legend says that two French men o'war, one a 74-gun ship, the other a frigate, approached the islands c1805 with the possible intention of landing troops on Scilly. At night, they apparently mistook the channel when they tried to creep in under cover of darkness and missed, but the larger of the two struck the rocks at the back of St. Agnes and foundered with all hands in deep water. This may be a confused version of the French warships lost 10.02.1781.

Harvey, a brig, was wrecked.

27 February. 'Sailed the *Evening Star*, master Tregarthen, for Penzance and from thence to Torbay to take up the guns and anchors of the *Venerable*, 74 guns, with a Mr.Tonkin of Penzance, authorised by Government for that undertaking.' (see 28 June & 30 July; Mr. Tonkin was an early diver, who the same year worked the wreck of the East Indiaman *Earl of Abergavenny*, off Weymouth).

Early March. A large quantity of nuts was found floating amongst the islands, presumably from a Spanish wreck.

28 June. 'Sailed the *Daniel*, master Duff, for Torbay, to take up the remaining part of the *Venerable's* guns, as a great part of them have already been taken up by the crew of the said vessel.'

30 July. 'Came in the *Daniel*, master Duff, and the *Evening Star*, master Tregarthen, from Torbay, having taken up all the *Venerable's* guns(on the 26th), except a few which lie under a raft of the wreck.' (Sunk only the previous year, were the iron cannon from the *Venerable* brought to Scilly to fortify the Garrison?)

29 August. 'Sailed the *Insolent* gun-brig, Lieut. Morris, with 66 men and 30 women and children from the *Pandour* lazaretto at St. Helen's Pool.' (A 5th rate man o'war named *Pandour* was transferred to HM. Customs as a store hulk in May 1805, and is believed to have been sent to Scilly as a floating quarantine hulk).

14 November. *Perseverance*, master J. Walker, a brig from Belfast to London, was wrecked on the Seven Stones. The crew reached St. Mary's in their own boat.

1806 – 10 January. *Governor Milne,* master Moffatt, Grenada to London, which had been captured on passage by the Spanish privateer *St. Pedro,* then retaken by the privateer *Minerva,* of Guernsey, put into Scilly with the loss of her rudder and other damage, and drove on the rocks. Her 135 hogsheads of sugar cargo was taken out to lighten her and she was got off.

Unfortunately for Mr Sickley, the prizemaster, she again went ashore at New Grimsby, the remains of her cargo discharged for the second time, and the vessel condemned.

April. 'The harbour of St. Mary's is glutted with privateers in miniature, some armed with swivels, some with musketry, and some with stones, all in pursuit of Prussian Eagles.'

12 April. *Brave*, Commander Edmund Boger RN. A 3rd Rate man o'war of 1,890 tons, 74 guns, was captured from the French in February off San Domingo, but suffered severe damage in the action. Temporarily repaired, she set out across the Atlantic in a leaky state. Her crew worked the pumps constantly, even French prisoners being released to assist. Most of her guns and 800 round shot were thrown overboard, and in a gale she rolled her mainmast overboard tearing up deck planking, breaking her gunwhales and boats. Her crew were taken off by the 3rd Rate *Donegal,* and the *Brave* abandoned. Wreckage from the ship drifted ashore amongst the Western Rocks and St. Martin's.

17 April. *Betsy*, a sloop from Leith to Lisbon, was wrecked on Southward Wells.

9 December. *Virginia De Carmen,* master Manuel, of St. Sebastian, from Vera Cruz to Cadiz, prize to the *Minerva,* a privateer of Greenock, master McKinlay, described as 50 ton lugger, was lost on the rocks at Scilly. Her cargo of silver specie, indigo, cochineal and many other valuable articles, the property of the passengers, was entirely lost. Only the captain and one sailor survived; four bodies were taken up and buried.

1807 – January. *Signora Carmina,* a prize vessel, and the *Nostra Signoa*, were lost amongst the Western Rocks.

March. *Duck*, master Billing, Padstow to Falmouth, went ashore and filled.

6 March. *Mary*, a sloop of Fowey, carrying oak timber, sank off Scilly. Crew saved but were picked up almost frost bitten by St.Agnes' pilots and brought to the islands..

25 May. One of a fleet of transport vessels carrying men of the German Legion, was lost on the Seven Stones. Only four or five men saved.

Early July. *Hope*, master Slater, a Plymouth vessel from Waterford to London carrying 800 sides of bacon; 80 casks of butter; 45 firkins of tongues; 20 tierces of beef; 15 tierces of pork etc. struck a sunken rock at Scilly but reached St. Mary's before sinking, where her cargo was sold by auction on 1 August.

25 July. *Catherine*, master Mason, a West Indiaman from Jamaica to London, ran on Rosevear Rock. The crew were saved, along with some of the rum and logwood cargo, but the sugar was lost. The hull of the ship was towed off and into St. Mary's Pool, with considerable damage. 500 gallons of rum and 600lbs of damaged coffee was sold by auction on St. Mary's on 7 November.

October. *Mayflower*, master James Crocker, a 29-ton Penzance sloop, built at St.Mary's in 1794, was lost with all hands near Scilly.

15 November. The brigs *Ann*, master Langdon, of Plymouth, and the *Tamar*, master Bevans, also from Plymouth on passage to Cork, were both wrecked on Tresco during a gale.

20 November. *Unity*, master S. Francis, of Teignmouth, from Bristol to Plymouth went ashore at Scilly and was sufficiently damaged to necessitate discharge of all her cargo at St. Mary's to effect repairs.

22 December. *Harriet & Ann,* master Wilkins, foundered off Scilly, all her crew being saved. *Swallow*, master Painter, a brig carrying copper ore from Cornwall to Wales, was lost on Scilly.

23 December. *Factor*, master Allez, an American ship from Valentia, was boarded off Scilly by a French privateer, her crew plundered the cabin and stabbed two of the crew. The *Factor* was then detained by HM. gunbrig *Strenuous* and sent into Portsmouth.

30 December. 'A duel was fought on St.Mary's Green by two officers, names unknown, of the *Royalist* transport, from Buenos Aires to Portsmouth; two pistols were discharged without effect, the parties returning to the Hotel to breakfast in good fellowship.'

1808 – 19 January. *Courier*, master P.Webber, a brig from Newfoundland to Dartmouth, was lost off Scilly with all hands.

Early February. 'Married at St.Mary's, Mr.Barnet Banfield, shipbuilder, to Miss Ann Nicholls, of the island of Trescow(sic).'

30 May. 'One of the *Colossus's* guns has been taken up this week, in a perfect state as if never underwater, by the help of the water glass, whereby any object can be seen 10 fathoms underwater; the Colossus has been

lost ten years.'

20 December. A brig went on the rocks during a heavy NE gale.

1809 – January. *Clarendon*, from Prince Edward Island for London with timber, was wrecked off Annet.

4 January. *Nancy,* master N. Goss, a brig of Plymouth, homeward bound from Llanelli with coal, struck on St. Helen's Island, and sank immediately in deep water whilst attempting to get into Scilly.

22 January. *Orion*, master Martin, a transport for Spain, was driven on shore at Scilly. The *Margaret*, master Martin, from London to Oporto, put into Fowey on the 25th after being on shore at Scilly.

6 March. *Good Intent*, master Le Fevre, Waterford to Lisbon, filled with water and sank after striking the Woolpack Rock. She was later raised and towed into St. Mary's, but condemned as a wreck.

4 May. *Hugh,* master McCoy, bound to Liverpool, was lost at St. Mary's.

3 November. *Commerce*, master Rands, Gibraltar to London went on shore at Scilly and had to discharge to repair.

19 November. *Ranter*, master Thomas, Cork to Falmouth and Plymouth, struck on some rocks at Scilly and sank in 20 fathoms. She was later raised and towed into St. Mary's, her crew and cargo being saved.

23 November. *Nymph,* master William Turner, a brig of Poole carrying cod fish from Newfoundland to her home port, was wrecked on Samson. The crew were saved but returning to their vessel next day found the ship had been stripped by men from Bryher and Tresco, everything moveable having been taken. 'Even the wearing apparel of the master and seamen had been carried off. The inhabitants of Bryher, we are told, distinguished themselves in this inhuman and infamous business. We shall not enlarge on the enormity of this barbarous practice, at present; but as the season has commenced, when, unhappily shipwrecks are frequent on our extended coasts, we request that on all such occasions, some intelligent person will send us the names of all those worthy men who distinguish themsleves by their exertions in saving the lives and property of the unfortunate mariners, and we will not fail to give the world the opportunity of knowing and admiring their generous conduct. We request also to be informed of the names of all such as shall render themselves infamous, on

these occasions, and we pledge ourselves that nothing shall deter us from holding up the names of such wretches to the contempt of all mankind.'

5 December. *Fortuna,* master Merritt, Minorca to London, went ashore at Scilly.

12 December. *Sulterton*, of Dartmouth, to Bristol, went ashore at Scilly and had to be repaired before she could proceed.

1810 – 27 January. *Perseus,* master Leigh, from Martinique to London with sugar, was lost at Scilly, probably near Samson. About 200 barrels and 80 hogsheads of sugar saved. Sale of the sugar (for exportation only because of the excise laws at that time) was held on St. Mary's in May, June and August that year.

15 March. *Orion*, master Mitchell, from Haiti to London, parted her cable in a gale and went ashore on Samson. Her cargo of mahogany was saved, and the vessel was got off and worked into St. Mary's Pool. It was reported on 20 March that 130 coasters were lying at Scilly.

14 April. Notice of the Act of 48th George III, requiring all ships entering or leaving Scilly to be navigated by licensed pilots only, after 27 March 1810. The names of the pilots appointed at Scilly are as follows, viz:-

Samuel Jenkin	Richard Thomas	John Wood
William Tregarthen	William Nance	James Tregarthen
John Thomas, snr.	John Jenkin	John Tregarthen

18 August. 'Died on the 5th instant of a decline, aged 36, Lieutenant Charles Williams, of HM ship *Hornet*, guard-ship at St. Helen's Pool, Scilly.'

31 August. *Amelia*, master John Craige. Of London, this full-rigged ship armed with 6 x 12pdr guns, carrying sugar, coffee, cotton and rum, was lost on Crebawethan, in the Western Rocks. Her cargo was saved, except for one cask of rum, six bales of cotton, six bags of coffee, a box of silver and another box of silver dollars.

22 October. An unidentified West Indiaman carrying coffee was lost at Scilly during the night.

3 November. *Harriott & John*, master Baker, from Waterford to London, got on shore on the rocks of St. Agnes, but was towed clear and taken to St. Mary's. Her cargo was saved but the vessel lost.

7 November. *Hope,* master George Craige, of Dundee, from St. John's was in great distress off Scilly, having lost her foremast, bowsprit and maintopmast, and one seaman drowned.

Reward, master Hammond, a brig of Exeter, from Limerick for London with oats and butter, was lost on the Seven Stones, and went down in about half an hour. Crew saved.

25 November. An unidentified French privateer, a prize to the 44 gun *Endyminion*, from Cork, ran foul of the 18 gun *Helena* in a gale off Scilly and stove in her bows. She filled and sank in 15 minutes, her crew being saved and landing on St. Mary's in the *Helena.*

1811 – 1 January. *Arcade*, master Gardner, from Bristol to Falmouth and Jamaica, went on shore on Scilly but was got off without damage.

2 January. *Isabella & Ann*, master Barclay, from Cadiz and Falmouth to Bristol, drove ashore on Scilly but was got off without damage. Her cargo was landed 'much injured, having been under water'.

12 January. HMS *Pheasant,* a sloop of war, fell in with the schooner *Nancy,* of Guernsey, off Scilly, laden with brandy and bound from Tarragonna to Falmouth. There were no persons on board, and it appeared from her logbook that she had for some days been in possession of the French and from the circumstances, there having been a violent storm the preceding day. It is supposed all the men were washed overboard.

7 February. *Francisco*, master Gelle, from Malta and Messina to London, drove ashore. Part of her cargo was saved, and with the ship's fittings was auctioned by Messrs Wilcocks & Edwards on St. Mary's on 8 April. The sale included two bower and one kedge anchors; eight muskets, a brass lamp, two compasses, a copper pump, the ship's bell and windlass etc.

In late February, wreckage, including tallow in casks, deal boards and a bale of cotton, was picked up, and a mast and rigging found floating off St. Martin's.

April. A large vessel has been seen floating bottom-up, about 4 leagues westward of the islands, but it was not possible to identify her.

9 June. *Intelligent*, Lieut. Tucker RN, ' - came into Scilly and by a bad pilot ran aground on a ledge of rocks, remaining there all that tide, until got off with the assistance of islanders with little damage.'

1812 – 26 January. *Maria*, master Thomas Jones, a galliot from Liverpool to Oporto with a general cargo, drove ashore on Tresco Island. An auction of her cargo took place on 29 April on St. Mary's, when some of the items sold were: 3,668 bundles of rod iron; 1,424 cast iron pots; 166 kegs of shot; 592 coloured woollen cloths; 550 pieces of long cloth and 80 barbozetts; 86 pieces of Manchester velvets; 179 firkins of butter; 1 case of cabbage seed; 449 bundles and 507 skeins of cotton yarn; 3,375 spells of cotton yarn; 2 cavalry saddles; 1,012 pieces of printed calico; 16 bags of loose coffee, 47 dozen files, 2 cases and 1 box of hats etc. etc.'

21 February. A vessel laden with oranges, with pieces of fruit boxes marked with the letter 'A', supposed to be Spanish, of 60 or 70 tons burthen, was lost on Scilly.

26 February. *John & Mary,* master C. Walton, a brig of 134 tons from Oporto to Cork in ballast, was lost on rocks in Broad Sound.

14 April. *Dispatch,* a packet vessel from Malta to Falmouth, was lost on the Western Rocks. Crew, passengers and mail all saved.

17 October. 'A pilot boat from Scilly, was upset last week in boarding a vessel, and Mr. Henry Nance, a branch pilot, was unfortunately drowned.'

2 November. *New Friends*, master Arnold, carrying wine and brandy for Liverpool, was wrecked off Scilly.

7 November. 'We have been favoured with the following list of Cornish names, extracted from the Report of the Committee for the relief of British Prisoners held in France' :-

S. Tregarthen, master of the *Mary & Betsey*, of Scilly.

James Bower, seaman of the *Nancy*, of Scilly.

William Chappel, mate of the *Adventure*, of Scilly.

James Tregarthen, master of the *Adventure*, of Scilly.

4 December. 'Genteel accommodation for passengers, to or from the islands of Scilly, combining conveniency with dispatch, the beautiful smack *Lord Wellington*, commanded by Captain John Tregarthen; which vessel is just off the stocks, and has been fitted up with every conveniency for the comfort and ease of passengers; sails from Penzance every Thursday between the hours of 9 and 11 every morning, for St. Mary's – and leaves that place for Penzance on the Monday following about the same hours of the day. Takes goods or parcels of any description, not

being contraband, at the most moderate freight. Captain Tregarthen may be found at the Dolphin Tavern, Penzance, any time between the arriving and sailing day.'

16 December. ***Thomas & Sally***, master R. Martin, 81 tons, Waterford to London was lost on Scilly, but her crew and two thirds of the cargo saved.

1814 – 13 January. ***Mary,*** master Brougham, a ship from Oporto to Liverpool with wine, went on shore on Scilly, but after cutting away her mainmast and discharging part of her cargo, she was got off and taken to St. Mary's Quay. ***Richard,*** master Lloyd, a brig from Chepstow to Plymouth with timber for Devonport Dockyard, went on shore on Scilly but was saved. At the same time the ***Montague*** packet went ashore, cut away both masts and was able to get off without damage to her hull. She arrived at Falmouth on 28.02 under jury masts, having been on shore and received much damage.

February. A vessel was seen to be on fire one night about six miles to the SE of Scilly, and was believed to have sunk.

4 April. 'For sale by public auction at 11 o'clock in the forenoon, the brigantine ***Brown,*** Dutch built and free, with all her stores and materials as she now lays in St. Mary's Pier. She is well found in anchors, cables, sails, rigging and materials, all of which are nearly new and will be sold in different lots. She stranded in St. Helen's Pool within the said islands, on her passage from Yarmouth to Dublin. For viewing apply to the master on board, or William Smith esq. the owner at Edwards Hotel.'

5 May. ***Hope***, master Allen, a sloop of Fowey, from Swansea with coal, was lost on the Seven Stones with her master, crew and passengers.

11 July. Public Wreck Auction at St. Mary's. 'At 11 o'clock, free of duty for payment of salvage charges, about 800 gallons of Port wine, in full and ullage pipes, being part of the cargo of the ship ***Mary***, stranded within the Islands of Scilly.'

4 September. ***Herald***, master Radley, a transport vessel from Lisbon, put into Scilly 4th instant in a leaky state, having struck on a rock.

26 September. ***Chance,*** a brigantine of Jersey, was found abandoned at sea by pilots belonging to St. Agnes and taken into St. Mary's where she was offered for sale by auction at the Custom House on Scilly on Monday

27 March 1815.

2 November. **Hope,** master S. Bartlett, a snow of 136 tons, Lisbon to London with wool, struck on a rock at Scilly and immediately filled. Her crew were all saved, also her cargo which was much damaged. The vessel went to pieces and her remains were sold for £40.

19 November. **Good Intent,** master Tamlin, Newport to Teignmouth, was taken and burnt off Scilly by the privateer **Lawrence,** of nine guns and 70 men.

23 November. 'Died at St. Mary's, aged 56, Mr. Barnet Banfield, ship-builder.'

1815 – 6 January. **Roscius**, master Omand, from Cork to join a convoy for Brazil, struck on the rocks off St. Martin's, broke her rudder and damaged her bottom.

8 January. **Perseverancy,** master Sly, from London to Belfast, put into Scilly having broken the pintles of her rudder by striking the bottom in St. Helen's Pool.

14 January. Four young men went out from Tresco in a small boat to pick up floating wreckage, when the craft upset and they all drowned.

27 January. **Queen Charlotte,** master Rayside, from Greenock to Jamaica with a general cargo, mostly cottons, ran ashore on Scilly Rock and was totally lost. Three passengers and one seaman drowned, the remainder of the crew, thirteen in total, managed to reach a rock where they remained without food and exposed for two days and a night, the sea running so high no boat could reach them. It was 29 January before any rescue attempt could be made by men from St. Mary's, when a Charles Jackson and James Tregarthen drowned, the accident being caused by ' – a heavy wave bursting with tremendous violence on the boat, overwhelmed it, and hurried two islanders into eternity'. The former had only recently married, the latter leaving a wife and nine children, and had lately returned from eight and a half years captivity in France after being taken prisoner as captain of a new St. Mary's built brig, the **Adventurer**, on 1 May 1806. The cargo of the brig was valued at £60,000, and was auctioned on 10 May, and contained such items as 3,271 Scotch cotton handkerchiefs, 673 pieces of striped calico; 71 white shirts, 25 check shirts and 38 dozen

pairs of white stockings.

13 March. *Sea Nymph,* master Denham, Portsmouth to Madeira, with fish and oil. She parted both cables and ran ashore on St. Mary's, her crew being saved. All of her cargo except some potatoes was saved.

Late March. *Margaret & Elizabeth*, from London to St. Michael's, was lost on St. Mary's.

September. *Jackson*, a snow from Oporto to London, was wrecked amongst the Western Rocks. Two boats from St. Agnes saved sixteen men.

29 October. *Thais*, master Appleby, Swansea to Penzance with coal, slipped her cables and ran ashore on St. Agnes, but was got off.

Ardent, master Lloyd of Cardigan, from Waterford to London, drove ashore during a gale on Annet, and was abandoned by the crew. They returned next morning and found that 300 firkins of butter were missing. She was refloated and taken to St. Mary's.

Elizabeth, master Mitchell, from Le Havre to Liverpool, drove on the rocks near St. Helen's, but was got off and carried into St. Mary's.

1816 – Early January. The finding of deals, spars, and a hen-coop and other wreckage indicated that a vessel had been lost within the islands.

4 October. *John,* a British vessel, London to Constantinople, was lost on Scilly.

10 October. *Barbados*, master Parry, of Liverpool, Smyrna to Liverpool with a valuable cargo, was lost on the rocks of Scilly. Her captain and fifteen crew took to two boats, but shortly after both upset and all drowned. The only man who elected to stay on board was Chief Mate C. Grumley, who having watched the captain and crew drown, made a small raft on which he was driven out to sea before being picked up two days later by a French vessel and landed in France, or, according to a different account, at Weymouth.

9 November. *Henrietta*, master Perry, from Swansea, and the *Edward*, master Banfield, of Scilly, from Malaga, parted their cables and drove on shore during a tremendous gale at WNW. The former was got off on the 11th , but driven on shore again at night during another heavy gale. Both were eventually saved and carried to St. Mary's Pier; the former had con-

siderable damage and must discharge, the latter only trifling damage, and was sent to Milford.

9 December. *Mary,* master Burstall, from Rio de Janeiro for Liverpool, having experienced severe weather on passage unshipped her main boom and left it on deck. Thinking that she was in distress from the want of after sails, two large sailing boats and the Old Town gig *Cuckoo* with sixteen men on board put out in heavy seas. The gig capsized and only prompt assistance by the other boats saved nine of the men. The *Mary* later drove ashore on 12 December and was totally lost with all her cargo. A bag of letters was saved from the wreck, handed to the Post Office and duly forwarded.

1817 – 2 January. *Eliza,* lost in the Isles of Scilly.

2 August. *Linnet,* a sloop of Cardigan, anchored near Crow Bar waiting the tide to enter St. Mary's, but dragged, struck and capsized. The crew were saved.

October. An unidentified vessel carrying wine and cork, was lost near Scilly during a series of gales.

8 December. *Susannah,* a sloop of Beaumaris, London to Westport carrying furniture, was lost at Old Grimsby, Tresco. Also the Custom House boat and a pilot boat sank at their moorings in St. Mary's Road.

23 December. *Isabella*, master Orress, London to Newport, struck the Seven Stones and sank. Crew saved and arrived at St. Mary's.

1818 – 5 January. A St. Agnes cutter with a crew of four put out to a vessel some distance offshore. Nothing more was heard of her and she presumably foundered in a gale that blew up that night. 'Moses Hicks, one of the men on board, had left a wife and family in the utmost distress'.

3 May. Four St. Agnes fishermen were drowned when their boat sank.

14 December. *Eliza*, London to Chepstow, foundered off Scilly.

1819 – 30 January. *Betsey,* master Coggin, Bristol to St. Michael's, was dismasted in a squall off Scilly. She was taken in tow by the *Lord Cathcart*, from Bengal, but the hawser parted and the crew abandoned her to be landed at Penzance by pilot boat.

12 February. *Olive,* master De la Bierte, Bristol to Ruan, sank near the Seven Stones. The captain and crew took to the boat and landed at St. Ives in safety.

20 March. *Mary,* master Harris, a sloop of Fishguard carrying oats from Youghall to Southampton, struck on the Western Rocks near Rosevear at night and was lost. Crew saved.

Early November. Pilots saw a sloop approaching the islands but she suddenly disappeared, and was believed to have sunk. Two weeks later part of the stern of *Sally*, of Workington, was brought ashore.

21 November. *Mary*, master Didgean, 'in a gale from N by W, from London to Cork, parted her cable and came on shore on the beach. She got off, but had to be re-caulked, being much strained. Eight bags of hops and some bundles of hoops are landed, being on deck. At the same time, the *Betsey*, master Phillips, from Newhaven to Liverpool, with flints, drove on shore and broke her keel and must discharge to repair'.

1820 – January. *Shannon*, Newport to Dartmouth was wrecked.

21 January. 'Last night it blew a very heavy gale from NW. The vessels lying at St. Mary's Road all drove. The *Elizabeth*, master Mather, from St. Lucia, lost an anchor and cable and drove down Crow Sound without damage. The *John*, master Campbell, from Prince Edward's Island to Bristol, upset the pawls of her windlass, and both cables ran out to an end, and is on shore on St. Martin's with loss of rudder and bottom much damaged. Part of the cargo landing, to lighten her'.

28 January. *Union*, master Taylor, from Chepstow, ran aground in going into St. Helen's Pool and filled with water.

16 October. *City of Edinburgh*, master Godly, of Quebec, from St. John to London dragged her anchors from Samson to Little Crow Rock and badly damaged, fell over and bilged. She was brought into the Pool three days later but again dragged in a gale and went ashore. She remained there for six months until floated clear in April 1821. She was then towed to Falmouth and sold. The same day the *Catharine*, master Campbell, from Cork to Plymouth, went on shore at Scilly but got off 'with trifling damage'.

22 October. *Fanny*, the Preventive Service boat, of about 20 tons, drove

from her moorings in a SW gale and was wrecked on the rocks near Carn Thomas.

21 December. *John*, master Thomas, Waterford to London, ran on shore in St. Helen" Pool, but got off with assistance after discharging her cargo. She was carried into St. Mary's Pier the following morning, where the rest of her cargo was landed.

1821 – 21 May. *Horse*, a St. Mary's gig which put out in heavy seas with four crew seeking pilotage. One man boarded a vessel for St. Mary's Roads the others returned, but a heavy sea filled and sank her drowning three men. Wreckage was washed up on St. Mary's.

2 October. *Providencia*, master Tellerman, a Spanish brig of 150 tons carrying wool from St. Andero to Bristol. 'About 9 o'clock in the evening of Tuesday in thick fog, this vessel ran on a rock on the western side of St. Agnes and began to fill fast. About 12 o'clock the crew first saw St. Agnes light, and fired a gun, when a number of boats put out and saved all on board. At daybreak almost every boat and man that could be spared from the different islands attended, for the purpose of getting out the cargo, which was happily effected on the same day, the whole conveyed to St. Mary's, but in so damaged a state through exposure to sea and rain that although originally worth £10,000, its present value is not above one third of that sum'.

3 October. *Hero*, a Bryher boat worth about £300, was dashed to pieces during a storm while salvaging the *Providencia*. Twenty-six men on board took refuge on a rock and remained there all night.

4 October. *Lord Nelson*, a pilot boat of St. Mary's, sailed for Penzance with five crew and was never heard of again. She was the best and largest boat in Scilly. Some of the crew had large families.

November. The St. Martin's Preventive Service boat capsized in heavy seas returning from St. Mary's, all four crew drowned. They had just received their monthly pay which was lost; eighteen children were orphaned by the accident.

1822 – 4 February. *York*, master James Farthing, a schooner of Chichester, Seville to London was lost in fog with all hands amongst the

Western Rocks, near Annet. 'On Tuesday morning a dead body and several pieces of wreck were driven ashore on St. Agnes, and the following day three more bodies, together with a vast quantity of oranges. The bodies from the wreck were decently interred in St. Agnes churchyard, in coffins provided by the direction of John Johns, agent to the Duke of Leeds. Great praise is due the islanders of St. Agnes for the promptitude with which they exposed themselves to a most violent sea, in a fruitless endeavour to discover any survivors of the melancholy catastrophe'.

1823 – March. A Tresco boat capsized off St. Martin's in a squall. Nine men drowned.
Early December. A boat belonging to Scilly towed in a 14 foot long keel boat, with '*Chieftain,* of London' marked on the outside of the stern. nb. There is a *Chieftain* figurehead in the Valhalla Collection.

1824 – 23 April. *Scotia*, master Lenox, from the Cape of Good Hope to London, with ivory, wine etc, ' – broke her anchor and chain in St. Mary's Pool, and drove to Tresco, where she grounded. Although the weather was exceedingly tempestuous the whole of the following day, and considerable apprehensions were entertained of her becoming a wreck, a number of boats were early in attendance, and by great exertions she was brought off to a safer place in the Pool, where her cargo is now being taken out'.
17 November. *Cecilia*, an Amsterdam registered vessel of 500 tons, carrying coffee, cotton etc. 'Yesterday the flag being hoisted at the lighthouse on St. Agnes announced a wreck near that island, and several boats endeavoured to proceed to that spot, but little could be done from the tremendous seas that raged around the Western Rocks. It appears that a vessel has foundered or been dashed to pieces near Rosevear, and it is feared this shocking event took place during one of the stormy nights and all the crew perished. Pieces of ship's timber have been taken up, the heel of a bowsprit, part of a stern, coffee and cotton have been washed up. A piece of stern marked *Amsterdam* and one of the sails has the letters "M.T." on it, from which it is conjectured she is a Dutch East Indiaman, also a compass marked No.1 *Cecilia*.'
27 December. *Janus*, a barque of North Shields ' – laden with timber was

discovered waterlogged, and driving at random amongst the Western Rocks. Great numbers of boats of all sizes put off to her assistance, and after much difficulty was brought into St. Mary's Roads. When boarded there was no creature found in her but a dead dog, her sails blown to rags. The wreck has been purchased by some persons belonging to Penzance, by whom she is to be repaired, and arrived at Penzance from Scilly to undergo a thorough repair'.

1825 – 22 March. ***Commerce***, from Porthmadog to London, struck on a ledge at the entrance to St. Helen's Pool, and received so much damage she had to discharge her cargo to carry out repairs. The same day the ***Reval***, master Allan, North America to Newcastle, went aground in coming in, but received no damage.
September. The ***Sidonie***, was wrecked at New Grimsby.
2 November. ***Spring Flower***, master Thompson, of Sunderland, Memel to Milford Dockyard, struck on the Seven Stones at 5 p.m. and filled. At midnight she went on her beam ends, and the master and seven men took to their boat, leaving one man, named Peter Dockter, on her side, prevented from joining them by heavy seas. Shortly after both fore and mainmasts gave way, she righted herself and drifted NE all the way to Polgerth Bay near Padstow, with the man still on board. The ship's boat which had intended to reach Scilly, was washed on shore near Newquay empty, and it was presumed they all drowned.
19 December. In heavy gales several large boats drove ashore. The ***Elizabeth***, of St. Martin's, went down at her moorings with the loss of most of her materials.

1826 – 16 January. 'On Monday last a schooner in distress was seen bearing towards Scilly from Land's End, and two pilot boats were on the point of proceeding from Tresco to her assistance when she struck violently on the Seven Stones and disappeared immediately. Of course the crew were drowned, and it is conjectured that the vessel was laden with coal or iron'.
29 January. ***John & Ann***, master Critchell, of London, Cadiz to Hull, 180 tons, was lost near Tresco, near Kettle Bottom with all hands, and the pilot, William Jenkin of Bryher. Seventy four hogsheads and 32 pipes of

wine were saved, and the bodies of the pilot and six crew picked up and buried. A silver snuff-box, a silver pencil case and silver mounted penknife were found on one of the bodies. The wine was taken by HMS *Reynard* to Plymouth.

25 August. *Cherub*, the Penzance-Scilly packet, master Tregarthen, missed stays working into St. Mary's Pool and ran on the rocks, but got off the following evening with considerable damage, and went alongside St. Mary's Pier. The *Cherub* ran on rocks in Mounts Bay on 18 January the same year, but the weather being calm, got off.

1827 – 3 January. *Mary*, a Whitehaven brig carrying pipeclay, was towed into Scilly by local boats having lost all her sails. The pilots were rewarded with £65. On the night of the 11th she grounded on an anchor of the *Squirrel,* causing her to bilge, and her crew were obliged to throw all her cargo into the sea to save her.

12 January. A sloop was lost with all hands during a bad strom. On the same day, a brig in the Pool was badly damaged, and a pilot boat was wrecked on the rocks.

19 February. *Osiris*, master Schaken, a Dutch brig from Pernambuco to Antwerp with sugar, coffee and hides, struck on the Seven Stones on Monday. A boat from St. Martin's went out and helped the crew who were about to abandon ship, to keep her afloat and get her into St. Martin's Pool. She is said to be the only vessel to escape after striking these rocks. Her cargo was discharged with much damage, some of the sugar having entirely washed out. The Magistrates at Penzance awarded the salvors £100.

18 May. *Hope*, master Catt, for London, in leaving Scilly struck on Bacon Ledge and broke her keel.

9 September. *Twende Sodskende*, master Bache, Bilbao to Copenhagen, a galliot, is believed to have struck the Seven Stones then made for Scilly but sank four miles off Bryher. Her crew were rescued by a pilot boat and landed at St. Mary's. In a sinking condition her master had requested an East Indiaman in the Channel to take them on board but his request was refused, on the grounds that they might yet reach Scilly.

28 October. On the 16th of November, part of the log-book belonging to the Danish galliot *Catharina Maria*, master Fredrickson, from Newport,

was found in a broken chest washed ashore on St. Martin's. On 28 October she had been seen off Land's End, and it was thought she had been lost that night on the Seven Stones.

29 October. *Susan*, master Miner, of Boston, USA, Matanzas to Hamburg, with coffee, cotton and logwood, struck on the Seven Stones and sank within minutes during a SE gale. The crew were saved by the pilot boat *Hope*, of Tresco, except for a black man who could not swim and refused to leave the ship, and drowned.

1828 – January. Five of the eight man crew of a row-boat were lost when she upset near Golden Ball Bar.

8 January. *New Jane*, master R. Smith, a sloop of Whitehaven, was found wrecked on Rosevear Island, but nothing was known of the crew's fate.

November. *Prima*, a schooner from Liverpool to London with salt was wrecked.

7 November. *Egbertina*, a Dutch brig of Antwerp, from Cardiff, carrying 1,641 bundles of iron, and 1,356 boxes of tin plate, bound for Dort, was in collision during the night near the Bishop. Her stern was so damaged that her cargo had to be landed on St. Mary's, and was re-shipped between 19.02 and 07.03.1829.

9 November. *Experiment*, a Swedish man o'war schooner, was stranded in a creek at the back of Samson Island; £150 paid to pilots and others by the Swedish Government for saving the crew and the stores, the ship having dragged her anchors in a violent gale, but was got off by the pilots and taken to St. Mary's.

18 November. *Josephine*, a French brig, after receiving much damage on the rocks was also taken into St. Mary's for repairs.

9 December. *Comet*, master Wade, of Liverpool, from Yarmouth to Malta, with potatoes, put into Scilly but during the night in a gale broke the pawls of her windlass and went ashore within St. Mary's Pier. On the next tide she filled with water and became a total wreck.
She was afterwards sold and broken up.

1829 – 4 January. *Ocean*, master G. Hall, of North Shields, carrying coal, was discovered sunk outside Rosevear, two miles west of St. Agnes. 'A prodigious number of boats from the different islands immediately repaired to the fatal spot, but nothing was got up which could afford any clue to her name. She appears to be a brig with yellow sides and black ports, and will probably be broken up by the next gale from the west. She is supposed to have foundered during the violent weather of Sunday night; all the crew must have perished'.

8 January. A quantity of wreck went ashore between Sennen Cove and Garner's Head, and it is supposed some large ship was lost on the Seven Stones in a gale.

14 April. *Letitia Tennant*, master Sinclair, Limerick to London with wheat, during violent squalls broke her anchor chain and drove on Creeb Rock at the back of St. Mary's Island and bilged. 3-400 quarters of oats were got out dry, but with the sea now flowing into her it was feared she would become a wreck.

1 October. *Prosper*, master W. Poat, a French brig, Marseilles to Ruan was lost on Crow Rock.

Late October. 'A few days ago the bodies of three men were picked up floating near the Scilly Isles, one of them had a knife in his pocket marked R. Porter; they had boots and appeared as if from Newfoundland. It is supposed some vessel was lost there three weeks ago.

Late November. *Jules*, a French brig of Granville, was brought in dismasted and abandoned, having been run down by some unidentified vessel. Nothing was known of her crew or passengers. Three days previous, the crew of a brig were seen hoisting large packages out of the wreck. She was identified by letters and papers found on board, having recently returned from the Newfoundland fishery, arrived at Le Havre, landed her cargo and sailed again.

1830 – 19 January. *Hope*, master Alfred Noble, a London brig, from the Cape Coast of Africa to London, was wrecked on the north side of St. Martin's Head, after mistaking the day-mark for St. Agnes lighthouse. A Dutch officer, Major Bregganpauwer, his lady, a small black boy and a seaman, put off in a boat, but were killed when the mainmast fell on them. The bodies were buried in St. Martin's churchyard. Four hundred elephant's tusks, pepper and 100 casks of palm oil were saved, along with seven boxes of gold dust and a box of 1,000 dollars.

7 February. ***Borodino***, master Haines, a British barque from Sierra Leone with logs of hardwood, oil, oak, ivory and gold dust, broke both bar anchors in St. Mary's Roads in a WSW gale, and went ashore on Carn Morval. Her crew of 21, including Scilly and Milford pilots, was saved by the prompt actions of the gigs ***Blucher***, ***Champion*** and ***Dove***. She discharged to carry out repairs.

3 April. ***Mars***, master Halley, Yarmouth to Bristol, struck a rock in St. Mary's Pool, stove in her bow and had to discharge for repairs which took about a month.

27 September. ***Hope***, a local boat from St. Mary's to Tresco, over-loaded and badly handled, shipped a heavy sea and foundered. Five of the 14 persons on board drowned, and some of those saved were resuscitated only with the greatest difficulty. The survivors included the Rev. James Law, Minister of Tresco, and Mr. James, the Schoolmaster.

November. ***Crompton***, master Burn, Llanelly to London, struck a sand bank coming round St. Martin's Head, but got off next day very leaky and had to be re-caulked.

27 November. ***Eugenie***, master Bensit, from Cardiff to Rouen, in coming to anchor at New Grimsby, drove on a ledge of rocks but was later got off with little damage.

29 November. ***Desire de la Paix***, master Kurno, a French chasse marie, from L'Orient with salt fish, ran on the beach in Porthcressa, having previously struck on a rock near Old Town Bay, her crew being nearly exhausted by fatigue. The wreck was sold on 14.12.

5 December. ***Commerce***, master Ludlow, of Dartmouth, was found off Scilly by the ***Marlborough***, her mainmast gone and her sails in ribbons, her foremast sprung and the vessel in such a condition that the eight crew were induced to abandon and scuttle her. They were taken on board the packet in an exhausted state.

1831 – 3 January. ***Lebanus***, master Thomas Williams, a full-rigged ship, was totally lost on Scilly at night, her crew saved.

8 January. A St. Agnes pilot boat with six men put out to the brig ***Leveret*** when she made a signal for a pilot, but on reaching the vessel her boom struck and caused them to capsize. The six men all managed to swim to

the brig and got on board by means of ropes, but one of them became seriously ill.

22 January. *Regulus*, master Smith, Antigua to London, struck on the Seven Stones, but by great effort was kept afloat and reached the mainland where she was run ashore near Penzance Pier.

1832 – January. *Sackville*, master J. Hurst, Sierre Leone to Great Britain, was lost on Spanish Ledges.

21 January. The *Heela Jamieson*, *Heed* and *Porcia*, were all stranded on Tresco, but later refloated and saved.

7 October. *Dart*, H.M. cutter, drove on the rocks at Carn Thomas in a severe NNW gale, bilged and filled with water but later got off.

6 November. *Jubilee*, master Furse, from Plymouth to Newport, ran aground on Tresco after striking on the Seven Stones.

16 December. 'The mast of a vessel sunk among the Western Rocks was seen, and found to be a foreign vessel, supposed a sloop, laden with wine and fruit; in the evening she parted and went to pieces.

Five pipes of Malaga wine and some empty fig casks marked B.C. Pomps & Mirasson, Malaga, have been picked up'.

Late December. 'Last week the remains of a vessel, name unknown, with a cargo of iron bars was discovered near Jacky's Rock, St. Agnes. A few tons of iron had been brought on shore but due to difficulties it is feared only a small part will be saved. The cargo was auctioned on 5 September.

1833 – 21 January. A rowing boat belonging to St. Martin's put off with ten men to put a pilot on board a brig, but was struck by heavy sea near the Lion Rock and sank immediately. Six of the crew drowned, being T. Godard; Woodcock, John Nance, Odgers and two Ashford's. Godard, formerly a marine, left a large family.

Late January. A gig belonging to Mr. Tregarthen, returning from the brig *Emma*, capsized in a squall, and all the crew got ashore except John Mabey of St. Mary's, who could not swim.

13 February. *Forester*, H.M. 6th Rate man o'war, Lieut. W. H. Quinn, RN., Plymouth to Africa, anchored near Crow Bar, parted and drove ashore on Cruther's Point, St. Martin's. Her foremast was cut away, bring-

ing down her mainmast head. All the stores were landed and all her guns thrown overboard and on the 16th she was hauled off and re-anchored. She was then towed to Plymouth and repaired.

13 February. *Providence*, master Campbell, an East Indiaman on passage to Bombay drove from her anchors and went on Crow Bar. She remained there for two days when she was scuttled. After being in that position for ten weeks, she was floated off on 14.05 but sank in five fathoms near the same place. The wreck and fittings were sold by public auction on St. Mary's on 10 June.

14 February. *Lydia*, master Smith, Charleston to Liverpool, drove on the rocks in New Grimsby Harbour, unshipped her rudder and carried away her cutwater. She was later assisted off.

23 February. *Thomas*, master Edward Nicholls, a brigantine of Fowey, 122 tons, from Bury with coal, struck on Woodcock's Ledge during a SE gale and sank in seven fathoms. She was raised and beached in June.

8 March. A smack of about 80-90 tons struck on the Seven Stones and sank.

18 November. *Joseph*, master Eilloy, of Sunderland, carrying cast iron ingots from Cardiff to London struck on the Seven Stones and sank, her crew were saved.

17 December. *Brothers*, master Mosey, from Bristol to Limerick, stranded near Tresco, but got off and alongside St. Mary's Quay on the 21st where 234 tons of cargo were landed in good condition.

1834 – 24 January. *Fairy Queen*, master Christmas, in getting under weigh beat over a reef of rocks, knocked off her false keel and damaged her sheathing. She was assisted to St. Mary's Pier.

26 October. *Elizabeth & Mary*, master Welsh, Yarmouth to Bristol, struck the Seven Stones, received much damage and was beached 26th in Old Grimsby Harbour where she discharged.

23 December. *Loyal William*, master Fauvel, Glasgow to Bridport struck the Seven Stones and was beached at St. Mary's for repair.

31 December. *Julia*, master Lundt, Liverpool to Antwerp, in getting underway, struck the rocks and had to be run ashore on Tresco. 1,200 animal skins carried as cargo were damaged.

1835 – 19 January. *Mercurius*, master Esink, a Dutch East Indiaman of Middelburg, carrying coffee and sugar from Padang to her home port, drove ashore on the rocks under the Garrison and became a total wreck. Nearly all her cargo was destroyed. Crew saved.

27 July. *Glenaladale*, master Taylor, Llanelly to Antigua ran on the Seven Stones but got off.

21 September. *Experiment*, master Williams, from Poole to Newfoundland put in to Falmouth with damage having been ashore on the Seven Stones.

24 December. *Malta*, master Bell, struck Black Rock at the entrance to St. Helen's Gap and sank, crew saved.

1836 - 4 February. *Fame*, master Henry Nelson, Newport to Newcastle with cast iron ingots, was abandoned after springing a leak. Her crew were saved by the St. Agnes pilot boats, *Champion* and *Cyclops.* She drove ashore on St. Agnes and became a wreck.

27 March. *Prosperous*, a 29 ton cutter of Tresco, registered at Scilly and built there in 1830, drove from her moorings at Tresco and went to pieces on the rocks.

7 April. *Bassenthwaite*, master Mitchinson, a Maryport brig, Liverpool to Quebec with a valuable general cargo and crew of twelve, struck one of the rocks at the entrance to Broad Sound, probably the Gunners, bilged and sunk. The cook and a cabin boy drowned, the remainder reached St. Agnes in their own boat.

13 October. *Minerva*, master Francis Hicks, of St. Ives, Gibraltar to Bristol with wool, struck the Crebawethan and was lost. The only survivor got on a rock and remained there till next morning.

21 October. *Experiment*, master Richard Bransfield, Newfoundland to Poole, on her maiden voyage with fish and oil, was found off Scilly dismasted and waterlogged. She was boarded by St. Agnes men who found three crew alive who had been without food or water for two days. The master, mate and four seamen were found drowned in either the cabin or forecastle. She was taken to St. Mary's Pool, the bodies being buried on the island. Part of the stern of another vessel was washed up at Porth Hellick last week, marked *John Dunlop*.

3 November. *Scotia*, master Cormack, for Blyth, struck on the Seven Stones but got off and was assisted into St. Ives.

26 December. *Edward Charlton*, master Morrison, of Blyth, Pembray to London, 238-tons, struck Bartholomew Ledge and sank.Her crew were rescued by the *Juno*, *Unicorn*, *Ranger* and the Coastguard boat. Her broken hull was towed on shore at St. Agnes and sold.

26 December. *Sarah*, master Carpenter, from London to Llanelly and Patras, ran into St. Martin's Bay and struck on the sand, but was got off and taken into St. Mary's.

26 December. *Pensher*, from Archangel to Bridgwater, drove ashore in St. Helen's Pool but was assisted off leaking badly.

1837 – 16 May. *Golden Spring*, master Irving, a 316 ton barque of London, struck the Seven Stones in daylight. She suffered considerable damage and became leaky, but arrived in Penzance.

2 December. *Fly*, a Samson owned yawl, 18 tons, broke from her moorings, drove on the rocks and broke up.

19 December. *George Lockwood*, master McKenzie, of Scarborough, struck on the Western Rocks, drifted off and in a waterlogged state managed to reach Penzance.

1838 – 20 January. *Vigilant*, master Ballantine, Westport to Newhaven, struck a rock when leaving St.Helen's Pool and was assisted off leaking badly.

23 January. *Wye*, master Fleet, Cardiff to London with coal, drove on the Bar of St. Helen's Pool, but was assisted off.

14 February. *Twee Gebroeders*, master Potjewd, a Dutch galliot of Rotterdam, carrying cotton, goods and sugar from Surinam to Amsterdam, drove on the rocks at night and bilged, and went to pieces. Crew saved. The *Zorgen Vlyt*, master Berghus, Liverpool to Rotterdam also drove ashore on Samson Island, part of her cargo was saved. The *Catherine O'Flanagan*, master Phillips of Scilly, bound for Wales parted from her anchors and went on the rocks inside the new quay at Rat Island. The Sicilian brig *Amelie*, Messina to Antwerp with oranges and lemons, drove ashore on Tresco, but her thirteen crew were saved. The schooner *Victoria*

of Exeter, coming in without a pilot, got on Crow Bar where the waves swept right over her. The crew were taken off by the gigs *Bee* of St. Agnes, *Juno* of St. Mary's, and *Bull*. During the rescue, *Bee*, a new boat, capsized but no lives were lost.

25 May. The French barque *Osiris*, from Moninica for France with sugar and coffee, struck on the Crim and later capsized in St. Mary's Pool. The crew were saved.

26 May. *Deux Soeurs*, Brindejone master, from Guadeloupe for Le Havre, struck on a rock and, being in a sinking state, was run ashore, whereupon she fell on her side and bilged.

27 November. The French barque *Pacquebot de Cayenne*, master C.T. Many (or Muny), from Rio de Janeiro for Le Havre with coffee, hides, and wool, struck on the Hats and sank but her crew were saved. She was said to have been carrying a large sum of money in silver dollars.

17 December. The brig *Anthony,* of Scarborough, 245 tons, W. Headley master, from Gloucester for London, was lost on the Seven Stones. The master and three of the crew were drowned.

1839 – Late January. Gigs from Scilly picked up large quantities of American deals indicating that a vessel had probably been wrecked.

22/23 February. The brig *Louisa Hannah,* of Poole, 165 tons, H. Moores master, from Lisbon for Poole with oranges and wine, struck on the Ranneys at night and was lost with all hands. Twenty-five small casks of wine and some oranges were salved.

27 March. The schooner *Solace,* of Plymouth, master Barrett, from Lisbon for Plymouth with wheat, struck near Rosevear in fog and was wrecked, but the crew of five were saved. The next day a St. Agnes gig engaged in salvage was capsized by the heavy sea around the rocks and her crew had to swim for their lives.

4 September. The brig *Theodorick*, 142 tons, master J. Scovie, from Mogadore for London, struck on a ledge to the westward of the islands and sank almost immediately. The crew were saved.

6 September. The brig *Hope,* of Mogadore, with general cargo, was lost on the Bishop and Clerks, but the crew saved themselves in their own boat.

6 December. The French chasse maree *St. Vincent*, master Rio (or Ris), from Marans for Penzance with barley, struck on the Chimney Rocks near St. Martin's Head and was wrecked. The crew and most of the cargo were saved.

1840 – 31 January. The brig *Lady Louisa*, of London, master Henley, from Rio de Janeiro for Cowes and London with coffee, came through Crow Sound and drove on Guthers Bar. She became a wreck but the crew were saved.

February. The French schooner *Louise Gabrielle*, master Bougain, from St. Ubes for Boulogne with salt, oranges, and figs, was destroyed by fire near Tresco. The mate was taken into custody on suspicion of starting the fire but was subsequently discharged through lack of evidence.

4 February. The schooner *Symmetry* of Gloucester, master Annerson (or Aanenson), drove ashore in St. Mary's Pool during a violent north-wester-ly gale and was wrecked. The crew were saved.

23 February or 17 March. *Jane Ellen* of Beaumaris, master Hughes, from Bangor for London with slates, struck on a rock near St. Helen's and sank. The crew were saved.

28 February. A large schooner struck on the Seven Stones and sank instantly with all hands.

16/19 November. The French brig *Nerina* of Dunkirk, about 114 tons, master Pierre Everaet, sailed from Dunkirk for Marseilles with oil and canvas on Saturday, 31st October. Her crew consisted of seven persons: the captain, the mate, the captain's nephew (a boy of fourteen), and four men. On the 16th November, a gale forced them to heave to, about 33 miles south-west of Scilly, The brig lay until 19.00 hrs. under close-reefed maintopsail and balanced reefed mainsail. At that hour she was struck by a heavy sea and completely turned turtle. The only man on deck, Boumelard, was thrown into the sea and drowned. The three other sea-men, Vincent, Vanataure, and Jean Marie, were in the forecastle and two of them by catching hold of the windlass, hauled themselves up to the keelson, so keeping their heads and shoulders above water. Jean Marie was not so fortunate, and after several attempts to haul himself up, he was drowned. The bulkhead between the forecastle and the hold had been started, and the two found that they were able to crawl along the keelson among the cargo. As they did so they were amazed to hear voices. The sound came from other survivors in the cabin. At

the time of the accident, the captain, the mate (Jean Gallo), and the boy (Nicholas Nisssen) were below. They had forced the lazarette hatch and climbed up into it, where they had been for about an hour when the others joined them. Space was very limited and they were obliged to stoop as they sat owing to lack of headroom, while the water came up to their waists. Night and day could only be distinguished by the reflection of the light coming through the water and up through the cabin skylight. The second and third day passed without incident. They had no food and were obliged to chew the bark of the oil casks.

Want of fresh air threatened them with death by suffocation, so the mate worked almost incessantly for two days and a night endeavouring to cut a hole through the keel with his knife. Luckily the knife broke. Had he suc-ceeded the result would probably have been fatal as the confined air was helping to keep the vessel buoyant.

At midnight on the 18th, *Nerina* went aground at the bow and the stern dropped down so much that they were compelled to move further for-ward. While doing this, Vincent slipped through the lazarette hatch and was drowned. An hour later the mate went down to the cabin, as the water seemed to have sunk lower, in search of a hatchet which was usually kept there, but had to rush for shelter to avoid being drowned by the heavy sea. An hour or two more and the dawn of the 19th – the fourth day – began to break. Then through the cabin skylight, the captain saw the rocks on which they were fast. He leapt down to find that the quarter of the brig was stove in and, looking through the hole, he cried out: 'Grace a Dieu, mes enfants, nous sommes sauves! Je vois un homme a terre!' The man on the shore put his hand through the hole and yelled with fright as he felt it gripped by the captain inside. Other men quickly arrived, the side of the ship was cut open and the crew were set free after being imprisoned in the vessel for three whole days and nights. In another half-an-hour the return-ing tide would have sealed their fate!

The spot at which the vessel struck was Newfoundland Brow at the entrance to Porth Hellick. It transpired that two pilot boats, seeing the vessel upside down, had attempted to tow her in, but the rope breaking and bad weather coming on, they had given up the attempt, unaware, of course, that there was anyone still on board. Had they not taken her in tow, the wind and currents would have taken her clear of the islands. The body of Vincent was recovered and buried in St. Mary's.

2 December. The schooner *Plenty* of Exeter, master Gray, from Newport, struck on the Seven Stones. She was taken in tow by a pilot boat but sank about a mile from the Eastern Isles. All her crew were believed drowned.

25 December. The pilot cutter *Waterloo* of Scilly, about 25 tons, was struck by a sea and went down almost immediately. The crew escaped in their punt but were ruined by the loss of their vessel.

1841 – 4 January. The s.s. *Thames*, 500 tons gross, master Grey,   from Dublin for Plymouth and London, struck on Jacky's Rock (one of the Western Rocks) in the dark hours of early morning. There was no panic, despite the dreadful weather, and she held together for some hours before breaking up. Only four of the sixty-five on board were saved. She had been driven off course by a severe easterly gale with hail showers, and she became unmanageable, despite her sails being set, when her fires were extinguished by the shipping of a heavy sea. The St. Agnes boatmen distinguished themselves in saving three women, and five of the crew of the St. Mary's lifeboat received medals from the RNLI for meritorious service.

1842 – Between 11 and 14 February, the brig *William Preston* of South Shields, 160 tons, from Odessa with wheat, struck on the Western Rocks and was lost with all hands.

2 April. A schooner was lost on St. Agnes.

12 October. The steamer *Brigand*, 600 tons, master R.H.Hunt, from Liverpool for London with bunker coal and patent fuel, struck on the Bishop and smashed one of her paddlewheels almost into the engine room. The fires were quickly extinguished by the water which poured in, but being built in four tight compartments, only two of which were broken into, she stayed afloat for two hours before sinking. It was fortunate that there were no passengers on board, since her two boats were only just sufficient to carry the crew of twenty-seven.

1843 – 13 January. the schooner (or brig) *Emma,* of Scilly, master Percival, from Liverpool for Leghorn, parted her cables in St. Mary's Road, drove on the rocks, and was wrecked.

28 January. A vessel of about 400 tons, and the schooner *Douro,* of Liverpool, 200 tons, master I. Gowland, from Liverpool for Oporto, were lost with all hands on the Western Rocks. Four days later it was reported that the Western Rocks were strewn with wreckage, including four figure-heads.

24 May. A stern plank of a large vessel was picked up. The name *Byker* was pained on it in gilt. (The barque *Byker,* of Newcastle, 230 tons, is posted as missing in Lloyd's 1843 Register of Shipping).

21 November. The schooner *Challenger,* of London, 16 tons, master Jones, from Smyrna for London with fruit, struck on the Nundeeps or the Gunners and was wrecked. The crew landed from their boat at Bryher whereupon the island was put in quarantine.

1844 – 21 February. The Dutch barque *Nickerie,* of Rotterdam, master Haweg, from Samarang and Batavia for Rotterdam with coffee and sugar, was wrecked on the Western Rocks at about 01.00 hrs. Of the crew of nineteen, only the sailmaker, Simon Greve, and the seaman, Christian Soupe, were saved. They were rescued from Rosevear in the morning of the following day at considerable risk due to the tremendous sea that was running.

9 October. In a tremendous gale, *Mary & Elizabeth*, master Tregarthen, from London for Cadiz and Gibraltar with general cargo, was driven on the rocks in St. Mary's Pool and wrecked. The crew were saved with much difficulty by Dennett's rockets, without which all probably would have perished. The wreck occurred only three hours after a brig was seen from St. Martin's to founder with all hands.

5 November. The cutter *Defiance,* of Samson, 25 tons, dragged her moorings, drove onto rocks, and became a total wreck.

1845 – 9 May. *Herald*, master Scaddan, from Lisbon for Liverpool, missed stays in working up St.Mary's Sound in a strong north-north-easterly wind and struck on the rocks.

1 December. The barque *John Esdaile,* of North Shields, 347 tons, master George Jackson, from Green Island or Quebec for London, struck on the Gilstone ledges. She was towed into Smith Sound, full of water, and became a total loss. The crew and part of her cargo were saved.

1846 – 3 October. the tender *Eddystone,* missed stays after leaving Old Grimsby Harbour and drove on the rocks to the north of the islands. She became a wreck.

1848 – 18 January. During the evening the schooner *Eagle,* of Glasgow, master Scott, from Glasgow for Charente with iron and coal, struck on the Crim at about seven knots. She did not lose way, however, and cleared all the outer rocks. The crew had to abandon her an hour later as the pumps could not cope with the incoming water, and she sank to the west of the islands. The crew landed at St. Mary's at 02.00 hrs. the following day.
4 April or 3 May. The brig *Tancred,* of Sunderland, 350 tons, Oliver master, sprang a leak and foundered north of the Seven Stones light-vessel. Presumably she had struck on the Seven Stones.
23 June. the steamer *Gipsy*, 84 tons, in ballast, foundered to the west of Scilly. The crew were saved.
29 September. The schooner *Caroline,* of Barnstaple, master Cathay, from Newport for Tarragona with coal, struck on the Seven Stones, in thick weather, and was lost with all hands except for the mate who was rescued by a boat from the Seven Stones lightship.
25 December. the Swedish brig *Charlotte,* of Stockholm, 350 tons, master E. Stranvitz, from Gothenburg for Montevideo with deals and balk timber, was lost at 04.00 hrs. on Melledgan. The master, mate, and seaman, a boy and a passenger were drowned. The ten survivors were seen on Melledgan at daybreak sheltering in a tent which they had erected.
27 December. The barque *Palinurus,* of London, 300 tons, master Gorl, from Demerara for London with rum and probably sugar, was lost during a north-easterly gale with all hands on Lion Rock. Seventeen bodies were washed ashore and were buried at St. Mary's. The first alarm of the wreck was given by the cows belonging to Mrs. James Jenkins' father which were frightened out of their field by the flapping and tearing of her sails.

71 puncheons and 14 hogsheads of rum were picked out of the sea. Her figure-head is in the Valhalla Collection.

1849 – 13 January. 'A Vessel may have been lost during the night, some oranges and lemons, a beam, cabin ladder, etc, being washed up on the shores. Pilot boats searched in vain for a wreck.'
27 March. A schooner went ashore on a rock near Santaspery Neck. She belonged to Plymouth and had a cargo of wheat aboard.
29 July. A Vessel was lost during the night. Wrecked cargo, portions of the ship, and two dead horses were washed ashore.

1850 – February. The snow *Woodpecker,* of Bristol, master Cook, from Africa for Liverpool, was believed to have been lost with all hands on the Western Rocks. Her round-house and boat were picked up thus enabling her identity to be established. 395 casks of palm oil (part of her cargo) were also salvaged from the sea.
30 October. the Greek brig *Calliope*, master Consalapulo, from Odessa for Falmouth for orders, putting in with damaged rigging, struck on Bartholomew Ledges and was run on the Garrison shore to prevent her sinking in deep water. However, she was a total loss, the wreck selling for £22.50. The cargo was also lost.

1851 – 1 January. During a heavy south-westerly gale, the Austrian brig *Allessandro il Grande*, from Galway for Cardiff in ballast, parted three anchor chains in the roads and drove on the Mare Ledges at about 22.00 hrs. The crew and ship's stores were saved, but the vessel was a total wreck.
23 April. The brig *Amethyst,* of Exeter, master Owen, from Teignmouth for Quebec with china clay, struck on the Seven Stones at noon and foundered six hours later about seven miles from the Longships. The crew were saved by the *Mary Laing* and landed at Falmouth.
14 September. The Sicilian brig *San Giorgio* (or *San Georgio*), master Romano, from Gioja for Hamburg with olive oil, struck on the Crim, came off, filled and capsized. The crew were taken off her side shortly after the accident by *Galway Ark*, and landed at Scilly next day. Later the

The ss. *King Cadwallon*, of Glasgow, belonging to the King Line,
lost on Hard Lewis in the Eastern Isles on 22 July 1906 in fog.

Acknowledgment: Frank Gibson

derelict was towed into St. Mary's Harbour from 50 to 60 miles to the west of the islands, and £2,500 salvage money was shared between the seventeen vessels involved. She was repaired at St. Mary's and sailed again as the *Lion,* of Scilly, master E. Odger, owned by a Mr. Weymouth and others.

15 October. A boat returning to the Seven Stones light-vessel from St. Mary's with stores capsized in a tremendous squall. Two seamen from the light-vessel were drowned.

1852 – All that was ever found of the large East Indiaman *Agnes Ewing*, Liverpool for Calcutta, was a box bearing her name which was washed up on Tean.

13 April. the barque *Mary Hay,* of London, 258 tons, master Hogg, from Jamaica for London with rum, lime juice, pimento, etc, struck on Steeple Rock although a pilot was on board. She was run towards Samson and brought to anchor, but the pumps could not cope with the water pouring into her, and she filled and capsized during the night. The crew and several pilots narrowly escaped with their lives. The hull was sold as it lay under water for £72. She was raised the following week and beached before being broken up. Much of the cargo remaining on board was salvaged. Her figure-head is in the Valhalla Collection.

15 April. *Renown,* of Liverpool, from Bahia for Hamburg with tobacco and cotton, caught fire in St. Mary's Road. She was run to St. Mary's quay and scuttled in order to put out the blaze.

11 August. *Elizabeth*, master Roche, from Quebec for Cork and Newcastle, was lost on the north-western side of the islands. All the crew were rescued.

22 December. A piece of wood, fifteen inches long, with *Abeona* carved thereon in one and a half inch letters, was found on Tresco.

1853 – 6 January. A piece of wood, three feet long and six inches deep, with *Tiberias* cut into it and painted yellow, was found on St. Agnes. It appeared not to have been long in the water.

26 January. the schooner *Sarah,* of Brixham, 95 tons, master Couch, from Cardiff for Tenerife and Santa Cruz with coal, sprang a leak, and, falling

in with two Scilly pilot boats, was helped to the islands and anchored on St. Martin's Flats, where she sank. The hull, materials, and cargo were sold three weeks later for £33.

February. A head or stern board, with the name *Montezuma* carved on it and painted yellow, was washed ashore, together with the upper part of a schooner's mainmast or a barque's mizzenmast. The wreckage did not appear to have been long in the water.

24 March. The schooner *Sultana,* of Hamburg, master Schultz, from Baltimore with Indian corn, was lost at night with all hands on Guther's Island during a south-easterly gale with hail and snow. Very little of any value was saved. (According to one account, the Danish brigantine *Flora*, from Baltimore for London with Indian corn, was wrecked on Guthers Island on Good Friday, 1853, but it has been assumed that the original record was inaccurate and that she was *Sultana*).

12 June. The Maltese brig *Ambassador*, master Ellue, from Cardiff for Malta with coal, struck on the Seven Stones at 6 a.m. in fine clear weather, and sank in about fifteen minutes. The crew of eight got away in their own boat and boarded the light-vessel.

1854 – 2 February. *America,* of St. John's, New Brunswick, 938 tons, from Callao and Queenstown for London with guano, struck on the Seven Stones and sand in 40 fathoms about an hour afterwards. The crew were saved and landed at St. Ives by the pilot boat *New Prosperous* of Scilly.

8 February. the schooner *Catherine,* of Cork, 87 tons, from Kinsale for London with oats and a crew of five, became a total loss off Scilly.

26 June. The cutter *Belinda,* of Cardiff, from Cardiff for Cork with limestone, struck on the Bishop in thick fog and foundered close by. Her crew were saved.

3 July. The chasse maree *Providence,* of Kernevel, from Bas Indre for Cardiff in ballast, went ashore in fog on the south-east coast of St. Mary's. The crew were saved. The wreck was sold for £8.

November. Several pieces of light wreckage were washed ashore. One piece was part of a head or stern board richly carved in gilt with broken Greek characters which translated into the name *Sicilia* (or *Cecilia*).

1855 – 19 February. *Libournais,* master Chanvelon, a French chasse maree, of Nantes, Cardiff to her home port with coal, was wrecked near Guther's Island. She was sold with all her materials for £136. (A newspaper account describes her as a lugger, named *Sibournais*).

3 March. *Rosherville,* master Brabyn. A London brig bound for Jamaica with beer, wine and brandy, she caught fire in St. Mary's Roads at 5 p.m. while her crew were ashore. She was waiting in the Roads for a fair wind, having recently been repaired in Scilly. Her stern was quickly engulfed, giving rise to suppose the fire started in the cabin. Her masts went overboard, and at 1 a.m. her cables burnt through and she drifted ashore at Pendrathen, near the Creeb Rock. Much of her cargo was salvaged, including 300 bags of rice. The remains of her hull were towed ashore on Crow Bar and abandoned, her cargo being auctioned on 5 March. Originally a French prize, her figure-head is in the Valhalla Collection.

Late May. A launch belonging to the Sunderland barque *Mariner's Hope,* 324 tons, master James Wiskins (or Whiskins), was found in Broad Sound. This barque appears in Lloyd's Register for 1855, but was deleted for the following year, suggesting her loss.

30 October. *Diamond* master William Thomas, a Swansea schooner, Cardiff to Waterford with coal, was abandoned off Scilly in wind conditions ENE force 9 and was seen to founder. One man was lost.

1856 – *Chieftain,* a vessel of this name is said to have been wrecked on Hard Lewis and a figurehead, the bust of a man in full Highland chieftain dress is in the Valhalla Collection. A barque *Chieftain,* 293 tons, was built in Scilly by Thomas Edwards in 1846, but her fate is unknown. In 1967 divers found a large section of wooden hull near Hard Lewis, complete with copper fastenings, which remains unidentified.

31 March. *Lady Raglan*, a head board painted black bearing this name in white lettering, was found on Annet.

11 May. *Mentor*, master William Pearce, a Truro registered brig of 220 tons, Devoran to Swansea with copper ore, struck the Wolf Rock during fog. She got off but filling rapidly ran for the mainland until 5 a.m. when she was abandoned and sank. Her crew were picked up by the brig *George*, of St. Ives, without loss of life.

1 August. ***Superior***, master Legg, from Falmouth in ballast went ashore in Scilly, but got off on the flood tide without much damage.

28 August. ***Custos,*** master Daniel Shaw, a full-rigged ship of Liverpool carrying general cargo and a crew of 17 for Bonny, on the west coast of Africa, struck the Crim at 2 a.m. and sank in ten minutes. Her crew took to the boats and landed on St. Agnes. Her master had been drunk for three whole days prior to striking the rocks. An auction was held on St. Mary's on 2 October, organised by Francis Banfield & Sons, Lloyd's Agents, at which was sold: '31 pipes and 55 casks of rum; 25 bales of cotton goods; 49 boxes of soap; 191 muskets; 2 casks of gun flints; 136 barrels of gunpowder; 4 bags of manillas; two cases of matches, sails and fittings'.

5-6 December. A wash-stand, painted white, and several pieces of wood, apparently cabin-work, all new, were washed ashore. The wreckage had only been in the sea a short time, and it was believed that a vessel had been lost locally during the night.

1857 – 11 January. A violent gale from NW that morning caused the Customs' boarding cutter to part her moorings, which went ashore and became a wreck. The pilot cutter ***Pet*** also parted her moorings, drove ashore and was damaged, but later got off and repaired.

23 January. ***Hero***, master Morse, from Penryn to Scilly, sank just inside St. Mary's quay.

4 March. A stern plank part broken, carrying white lettering which appeared to read '***Firene***, Lymington', was found floating near the Seven Stones. Possibly from a vessel of that name.

21 March. ***Velox***, master John Thomas, a Cardigan registered schooner from Swansea to Dordrecht with railway lines and chairs, missed stays beating into New Grimsby Channel from the north during a ESE force 9 gale. She struck Shipman's Head and sank, only her master being saved from her four man crew, his life being saved by the crew of the pilot cutter ***Garland***, who received £4 from the Board of Trade. In a letter from the Chief Coastguard on Tresco to the Receiver of Wreck, St. Mary's, he commented 'this secret I may trust you with, that had the master taken a pilot when offered, it would not have happened'. The same day the ***Victorine***, master Deveux, from Cardiff with coal, drove on the rocks but was saved.

1 June. *Voluna*, master James Vowden, a 336-ton Padstow brig, Falmouth to Quebec in ballast, was lost on the south side of St. Agnes. The ship's boatswain was on watch at the time, and being foggy, a seaman was on each side of her bow as lookout when she struck. The Board of Trade Inquiry at Falmouth stated: ' – that the loss of the ship was caused by default of the master in want of knowledge of the tides and coast, and also to inaccurate steering, the course selected being too narrow to admit of any northerly variation. No culpability is apparent on the part of the master, whose conduct seems to have been seamanlike and steady'.

21 September. *Elspeth*, master John Francis Cull. A London barque of 282-tons, Newcastle to Martinique, foundered 35 miles WNW of the Isles of Scilly, after springing a leak. Her crew were saved by the *Euxine*, which brought them into St. Mary's Roads.

1858 – 12 February. *Diligente*, master Amicelle, a French schooner carrying coal, whilst shifting her berth without a pilot, got on a rock and filled with water.

7 May. A head board, painted blue with gilt edges, and the name *Royal Bride* in gilt letters was found on one of the Eastern Isles.

16 March. *Kingston*, master Arthur Clutterbuck, a barque of Hull, 286-tons, Shields to New York, suffered damage in a gale and put into Scilly for repairs. On completion, she was passing through the New Grimsby Channel when she struck the Hulman, lost her false keel and became leaky and had to discharge for more repairs.

15 September. *Clydevale*, master William Hesketh, an iron sloop of Glasgow, Paisley to London with castings, went ashore in Scilly and sustained considerable damage.

19 November. *Maria Whitfield*, master Shelley, foundered off Scilly whilst on passage from Cardiff to Southampton with coal. Her crew were landed at Penzance.

12 December. *Alexander*, master Francis, from Llanelly with coal, in entering New Grimsby, ran on shore near Bag's Ledge, but got off the following day, apparently without damage.

1859 – 9 February. A stern board was picked up which bore the name *Rosalie*.

9 April. **Siluria**, master Nance, sustained damage after having been on shore, but was assisted off by men from St. Martin's.

27 April. **Fame**, a Newlyn fishing boat, capsized and was lost with all hands near the Seven Stones lightship, whilst attempting to reach Scilly for shelter in an ESE gale.

14 September. **Caurinus**, master Tabo, of Padstow, struck the Wolf Rock whilst bound for Sidmouth with slates. She was abandoned in a sinking condition.

1 November. **Naomi**, master A. James, an Aberystwyth schooner, carrying coal for Girzenti, parted her mooring in the Pool and ran ashore on Porthmellon Beach. £50 was awarded the boatmen, particularly captain Jenkins of the **Star,** who helped take out her cargo and get her off, hawsers of 350 fathoms then being attached to the capstan on the pier, by which means she was warped off and got inside the pier.

19 November. **Duke of Wellington**, a schooner carrying oats from Waterford to Truro, was wrecked in thick fog and lost with all hands.

1860 – 30 January. **Adeline**, master I. P. Journes. A French brig carrying coal from Troon to Malaga, dragged her anchors in a gale, then slipped her cables in an attempt to reach the open sea, but drove on Sandy Bar and became a total loss. Her cargo was sold to the islanders at 6 shillings a ton. One of her anchors with chain attached was later taken up by Martin Ellis and the crew of the **Dan** and handed over to the Receiver of Wreck. In a gale 'of awful violence' which swept over the islands, the Bishop Rock lighthouse was damaged and two vessels drove ashore, one of which was wrecked. The gale was from the west with a terrific sea, and at its worst during the hours of daylight.

31 January. **British Queen**. A schooner carrying bones from Rio Grande to Falmouth, was abandoned offshore with a leak, and sank within sight of the crew who had taken to the boats.

8 February. **Eagle**, master W. Jefferson, from Llanelly to London with coal, struck on a rock whilst lying at anchor and filled. She was later got off and towed to St. Mary's Pier with a hole in her bottom about 2 feet square.

13 February. **Endeavour**, master E. Evans, of Carnarvon, from Portmadog, was abandoned off Scilly, the wreck being towed into St.

Mary's harbour as a derelict by master Woodcock, of the pilot cutter *Queen*.

18 February. *Pauline*, master Halgand, a French schooner carrying railway iron from Ardrossan to Rouen, drove ashore in a severe gale on Crow Bar, but was later refloated and saved.

27 February. A stern board was picked up in Tean Sound bearing the name *Richard Brown.*

2 April. *Yaca*, a full-rigged ship of Greenock, carrying coal, was sighted offshore on fire, and watched until she sank.

14 July. *Osvetitel*, master C. Meilicich, an Austrian barque carrying barley from Ibrail to Falmouth, went ashore in fog at 10 p.m. on Maiden Bower. 'The wreck was not seen until next day, when the inhabitants of Bryher went to the scene and found the master, his wife and crew on the rocks. Fortunately the weather was moderate, and they saved nearly the whole of the stores and materials. The ship was fast breaking up and becoming a total wreck, so that nearly the whole of the cargo was lost. The stores have been taken possession of by Messrs. Banfield, the consular agents, and about 1,000 quarters of barley have been salved'.

19 August. *Aurora*, master Alessio Mulato, Ibrail for Falmouth with wheat, was wrecked at 2 a.m. in the vicinity of the Gilstone Ledge. The crew took to their boat and reached St. Mary's.

14 September. *Punjab*, master Dale, a Sunderland barque, carrying wool and hides from Port Elizabeth to Amsterdam, struck the Seven Stones and foundered within half-an-hour. There was scarcely time to launch her two boats, one of which tried to take on board all eight passengers, but the wife of the French missionary Rev.Arbousset, returning after 28 years in Africa, fell overboard and drowned in front of her husband and children. The crew and passengers were rescued by the brig *Joshua & Mary* and landed at Falmouth. The body of Mrs.Arbousset was found ashore at St. Columb Porth, on the mainland, on 7 October, identified by her rings and clothing.

3 November. *Alice*, from New York to London with wheat, flour, clover seed, rosin and staves, was abandoned off Scilly, and towed into St. Mary's derelict by the barque *Faithful*, of Ipswich, which saved the crew. She was later towed to London by the steam tug *Napoleon*.

26 November. *Empire*, master George Woodcock. This London paddle steamer, carrying coal from Greenock to Bordeaux, struck on Picket Rock at 1 p.m. during a severe gale, whilst attempting to enter Broad Sound without a pilot. A number of Bryher and St. Agnes boats went to her assistance, including the *Az* and the *Gem*. They found both of the *Empire's* lifeboats carrying thirteen crew, her master and carpenter still being on the wreck. These were later saved and taken to St. Mary's.

27 November. *Rapid*, a Falmouth schooner of 156-tons, from the Clyde to Dieppe, foundered 30 miles NW of Scilly.

31 December. *Elizabeth*, master Dangas, a French brigantine of La Rochelle, was towed into Scilly dismasted, carrying 140 tons of coal. She was sold by public auction where she lay alongside St. Mary's pier, followed by her materials. All 64/64th shares were then transferred to a Charles Newman, of Liverpool, and her registry transferred to that port from July 1869.

1861 – 6 January. *Joseph Howe*, Cardiff to Loando with coal, was abandoned off Scilly and sank, her crew being saved by the sailing vessel *Indus*, from Madras.

17 February. *Pauline*, master Truscott, Cardiff to St. Nazaire with coal, fell over and bilged, and it was expected she would break up. A second vessel also named *Pauline*, a French schooner, master Halgand, Ardrossan to Rouen with railway iron, drove ashore on Crow Bar and was wrecked. Part, if not all of her cargo was saved. nb. Despite the details of this wreck and the one preceding being suspiciously similar, according to Lloyd's List, they are two different vessels.

18 February. *Mentor*, master King, a schooner from Sierra Leone to London with palm oil and other cargo, parted both cables and drove across the French brig *Arthemise*, of Bordeaux, master Lemere, from Cardiff to St. Nazaire with coal, causing her also to go adrift. The *Mentor* drove ashore on St. Martin's, but was later got off and taken into St. Mary's, but the *Arthemise* went ashore on Tresco and is believed to have gone to pieces.

19 February. *Erne Hagemeister*, master Hermann, of Rostock, from Constantinople to Falmouth was seen to founder close to the islands. A

life-buoy bearing that name and letters in a seaman's trunk, helped to identify the wreck.

21 February. *Merlin*, master Hicks, of Scilly, London to St. Michael's in ballast, went ashore near St. Mary's and was wrecked. Her crew were saved by the rocket life-saving apparatus, and later her stores and materials. She later drove higher up on the rocks, was condemned and sold.

19 March. *Award*, master Watts, a salvage vessel of Liverpool, on passage to New Orleans, struck Gweal Rock, Bryher at 1 a.m. during a severe NNW gale. The crew were unable to get ashore over the fallen mainmast for 12 hours, after which they remained on the rock for a whole day until landed by Bryher fishermen. The ship's fiddle-head and quarter-board from this vessel can be seen in the Valhalla Collection. The other quarter-board was made into a sign for the New Inn, Tresco, and much of her timber went into the roof of the dining room of Tresco Abbey, and other rooms still named Rosevear, Rosevean and Annet. The teak sideboard in the dining room was made from the mainmast of the *Award*. James Jenkins was awarded three shillings for giving information of this wreck to the Coastguard.

4 April. *Cornelia,* master Woodside, a full-rigged ship of Portland, USA, on passage from Greenock to Santos, Brazil, with railway sleepers, two locomotive engines and coal, sprang a leak on 31.03 which increased. Despite pumping, she was abandoned 25 miles north of Scilly with 7.5 feet of water in her hold, and soon after foundered. Her crew were picked up by the schooner *Mary Ann,* which towed their boats to Scilly, where they cast off, landing at 3 p.m.

1862 – 11 January. *Dumbarton*, a paddle steamer on passage to Bahia, Brazil, was seen in difficulties near Potts Ledge, flying signals of distress in a heavy west gale. A boat from Bryher reached her, and after slipping both chains, she was run ashore at New Grimsby Harbour, but later refloated.

22 January. *Hudscott*. A Bideford schooner, Newport to Plymouth with coal, coming leaky and without a pilot, struck the rocks and made so much water she was run aground in Old Grimsby Harbour where she filled. Temporary repairs enabled her to be got to St. Mary's where her cargo was discharged.

24 January. *New Quay*, master Tinmarop, of Riga, foundered 50 miles WSW of Scilly on passage from Cardiff to Symrna with coal. Her crew were landed at Falmouth, by the *Little Western*.

24 January. *Alexandrine*, a Cardiff brig carrying coal, which parted her cables and was abandoned in the Roads in a gale. £97 was awarded to the pilots and boatmen for getting on board and running her on the beach at St. Martin's, and later for assisting her off and recovering one of her chains. The same day the sailing ship *Cater* of Ipswich, carrying railway iron, was also driven ashore at the same place, and £30 awarded to the boatmen and others for assisting her off the beach.

1 February. 'On Tuesday last week (04.02) the *Little Western* from the Scilly Isles, brought news of a steamer being lost on the Western Rocks at Scilly. Several pieces of wreck had come ashore and some papers giving the name of the steamer, which left Liverpool some days ago for the Mediterranean. The name had not been written down and had been forgotten. It was said that the steamer's lights had been seen, and that she struck on the Crim Rocks.'

29 April. *Hobard*, an American brigantine, ran ashore on Samson, but was got off and towed to St. Mary's Pier by two pilot boats. The greater part of her cargo of barley was saved, although damaged.

Marie Clemence, master Auray, Cardiff to Port Louis, in entering Scilly without a pilot, struck Queen's Ledge and knocked off her rudder and became leaky. She was beached at Hugh Town and had to unload for repairs.

29 May. The pilot cutter *Presto* picked up a six foot tall figurehead of a female, painted white with blue facings and a wreath of flowers around her head. It had apparently been in the water for some time.

16 June. A five foot six inch tall figurehead was found of a large gilded eagle, holding in its talons the American arms of a shield, which had not long been in the sea. Neither of these figureheads survive in the Valhalla Collection.

18 October. *Tower*, master Chalk, a Padstow schooner bound for Poole from Cork with oats. She put into Padstow leaking badly having struck the Seven Stones.

1863 – 17 February. ***Petite Angelina***, a French lugger of Vannes, was seen off Scilly some distance to the SW without sails and on her beam ends. Several men proceeded to her in a rowing boat and two sailing cutters. On reaching the wreck it was found she had been abandoned when her ballast shifted and her pumps choked. She was five miles SW of the Bishop Rock and was taken in tow and handed to the Receiver of Wrecks on St. Mary's. Papers found in her showed her master's name to have been Denis, and she was but a short time out of France. She was later sold and re-named ***Pride of the West*** and registered at Scilly.

20 May. ***Sarah & Emma***, a brigantine which struck on the south rock of the Seven Stones and went down with all hands. Parts of her topsides and stern were found off St. Martin's a few days later. She had formerly been the ***Bonne Maloinne*** of St. Malo

22 May. ***Scotia***, master Lang, a barquentine of Penzance, carrying coal, foundered 20 miles west of Scilly after collision with the ***Exchange*** of St. Ives. Her crew were saved by the Dutch brigantine ***Adrianus Johannes*** and landed at Scilly.

9 October. ***Porthcressa***, master Gibson, a ketch of Scilly, from Southampton with a cargo of ship-building timber, whilst beating into the harbour at Scilly at night, the weather very thick and dark, drove ashore on a reef of rocks and remained there for two days. She was got off after throwing overboard her deck cargo but suffered serious damage.

1 December. A French schooner grounded on St. Martin's Flats during a storm and later sank at anchor. Crew saved. ***Diana***, master Duff, a Southampton brig from Quebec to Southampton with timber and the brig ***Lavinia***, master Lord, of Newport, for Poole with coal, both drove ashore on Rat Island at the back of St. Mary's Pier. The crews were saved and the ***Diana*** refloated a week later, the ***Lavinia*** was dismantled for her timbers. Three of the crew of the ***Diana*** narrowly escaped drowning by foolishly leaving the vessel in a small boat at the height of the storm.

2 December. ***Adolphe***, master Vigoureaux, a chasse maree from Cardiff to St. Nazaire with coal, was in collision with the French schooner ***Anna & Egoda***, the latter having parted her chains, drove foul of the other vessel and did so much damage that she foundered in St. Helen's Pool where she lay a total wreck. She was 38 years old and valued at less than £100.

Euphemie, master Riteau, from Cardiff to Nantes with coal dragged her anchors and ran foul of a ketch, the *St. Helen's*, in St. Helen's Pool. The master scuttled the *Euphemie* to prevent her being driven against the rocks or out to sea. Her crew were taken off by a boat from the shore. The Falmouth schooner *Oscar*, master Howell, was driven ashore on Tean Island after dragging her anchors, but was got off by the 10th and taken to Old Grimsby Harbour without serious damage.

2 December. *Factory Girl*, master Thomas Tallistire, a Liverpool full-rigged ship carrying coal from Swansea to Valparaiso, which foundered off Scilly when struck by a severe NW gale causing her cargo to shift. Her crew cut away her mizzen and foretopmast, which in falling carried away her mainmast. Her mate, six seamen, the captain's wife and child were saved by the brig *Albatross*. The intention was for the boat to return to the wreck to save the remainder of her crew and captain, but before they could arrive she went down head first and every person left on board drowned.

Friar Tuck, master Tierney, a full-rigged ship of Liverpool, carrying tea from Foochow to London. One of some 500 vessels in St. Mary's Roads riding out a NNW hurricane, she parted her cables and drove ashore on Newford Island, where her crew cut away her masts after she struck. The rocket apparatus was used by the Coastguard to rescue 19 crew, four men getting ashore in a boat. More than 1,100 chests and boxes of tea, the equivalent of three small shiploads were saved, most of it completely saturated with water. The threat of plunder was such that Mr. Coll, the Receiver, sent to Penzance for 3 or 4 trustworthy officers and 'glutment'. Much tea was stolen and it is said it is still drunk on special occasions in the islands. 304 chests were saved undamaged, 93 part damaged, 750 saturated, having been submerged 6 or 7 weeks. Chinese geese now at Tresco Abbey are descended from those on board. The figure-head of the *Friar Tuck* is in the Valhalla Collection. In this wreck incident, Francis Banfield, of Messrs. Banfield & Son, Lloyd's Agents, and Mr. Watts, a blacksmith, were both badly injured. A cable from the wreck was taken to a capstan on shore, and when bar taut, a stopper was put on the cable to maintain the tension. Orders were given to withdraw the capstan bars, but two were left in. The wreck gave a sudden heavy lurch, the stopper gave way, the capstan flew round, throwing Mr. Banfield into the air and over the cliff, Mr.Watts received the full force of a bar just below the shoulder, which broke his arm and smashed several ribs. Dr J.G. Moyle attended their wounds and both men recovered.

1864 – 4 January. *Minna*. This brig of Blumenthal in Hanover, carrying timber from Quebec to Liverpool was found waterlogged, dismasted and derelict 25 miles SW of Scilly. It was towed into Broad Sound by three pilot cutters, but broke adrift and went out to sea, to be found four miles off by a steamer which brought her into St. Mary's Roads where she was valued and the salvors proceeded with a warrant in the High Court of Admiralty. *Agnese*, a French schooner of Granville, on passage from Llanelli with coal, collided in fog with the brig *Circassian* of Scilly and foundered, the brig landing the crew at St. Mary's.

2 May. *Aegir*, master Wendin. The sum of £150 was awarded the men employed in getting this Swedish brig off the rocks at St. Agnes, and for bringing her to St. Mary's Pier. She carried olive oil from Queenstown, and was discharged for repairs.

3 November. *Grootzeesjk*, a Dutch schooner which foundered offshore, her crew being landed on Scilly by the barque *Mary Hall.*

18 November. *Helen's Bank*, was left anchored in an exposed position with only three men and a boy on board, the master and remaining crew ashore ill with scurvy and diarrhoea. She dragged and went ashore on the north side of St. Mary's and lost her rudder, but later towed into the harbour by the *Little Western*. *Gephiena Helena,* master Vries, of Holland, suffered severe damage at sea and lost five crew washed overboard. The pilot cutter *Agnes*, of Scilly, assisted her to St. Mary's there being only one seaman, the master, his wife and child, left on board.

26 November. *Skulda*, master Tormessen, a Norwegian brigantine, put in to St. Mary's on 04.10 where her cargo of railway iron was landed on the quay so that she could be repaired. On completion her cargo was reloaded, but then she broke her moorings, went ashore on Porth Mellon beach, suffered severe damage and filled with water.

27 November. *Boadicea*. This Bridgwater schooner carrying cod-fish and oil from Indian Tickle, was found derelict by the pilot-cutter *Agnes* and brought in. The salvors excepted £530 for services.

1865 – 14 January. *Calliope*, a Norwegian barque carrying maize, was abandoned off Scilly in a sinking condition.

19 March. *Sarah*, master Pearce, a Devoran schooner, was abandoned 25 miles WNW of Scilly. Her captain and six crew were given up as lost but were later landed at Plymouth by a brig.

11 April. *Hercules*, a Swansea ketch carrying timber, was brought into Scilly derelict, stripped of her sails and running rigging.

29 April. A large brig of about 350 tons was seen to founder between Land's End and Scilly in a gale. One man survived clinging to a spar, and a passing vessel threw him a rope, but after being dragged through the sea for a while he let go and drowned.

1 May. *Zoe*, master Joseph Crisp, carrying zinc, was brought into St. Mary's by the *Babthorpe* of Colchester. Messrs F. Banfield & Sons, agents to the owners requested release of the cargo from HM. Customs Receiver of Wreck, on security that salvage may be due.

5/6 November. *Vigilant*, master Stockdale, a Scarborough dandy, Cowes to Galway with cement, was wrecked on Shipman Head, Bryher, at night in bad weather. Crew saved.

1866 – 6 February. *Hydra*, a Hamburg barque. £600 was awarded the crew of the rowing boat *Prince*, £800 to the pilot cutter *Gem*, and £1,000 to s.s *Little Western*, for assistance rendered.

13 February. *Dauphine*, a French schooner, Liverpool to Cette with pitch, caught fire ten miles off Scilly, causing the crew to abandon ship. The flames were seen from St. Agnes, and a local boat went and met the crew who were rowing for the island. At 2 a.m. the wreck burned to the water's edge on the south-west corner of St. Agnes. Only her masts and some rigging were saved.

24 March. *Harriet*, a brig of Ardrossan, carrying coal to Bordeaux. A letter in the Scilly Custom House records state: 'I beg to forward letters signed by James Jenkins, pilot on behalf of the crew of the pilot-cutter *Rapid*, requesting they be remunerated for landing three seamen from this brig which foundered off Scilly, three other crew being lost.

25 March. *Wealands*, master Stirling, foundered off Scilly.

12 April. *Gilmore*, master Duff, a Southampton barque, in ballast to

Quebec with a crew of 18, struck Hard Lewis, off St. Martin's and sank. The crew of the rowboat *Lively* were awarded the sum of £12, and the crew of the pilot-cutter *Queen*, £10.

25 April. *Cubana*, master Patrick, carrying coal and iron for Cuba, struck the Seven Stones at 2 p.m. in fog and sank drowning seven crew. Almost a new vessel, she was on her second voyage.

18 September. *Emilie*, master Johnstone, a Glasgow schooner, struck the Seven Stones and sank within five minutes, her crew remaining on the lightship unable to reach Scilly until 24.09.

1867 – 5 January. *Eliza*, master Collins, a Porthleven schooner carrying coal. A newspaper account records: 'At their own peril the steamer *Colon* lay by the sinking *Eliza* off Scilly for upwards of four hours, the ship's company cheerfully lending their aid to save the crew, where on reaching Liverpool, the two crews parted in the most affectionate manner'. nb. A small fiddle head of grapes in the Valhalla Collection is thought to have come from her. The same day, the flat *Gem*, carrying slate foundered off the Bishop Rock.

8 January. *Jeune Celestene*, master Thape, Swansea to Nantes with coal, went ashore on Little Ganinick and became a total loss.

19 January. *Vesper*, master Samuel Lindsay, a paddle steamer of Glasgow, bound for Brazil where she was to become a passenger ferry at Bahia. Off Scilly, some 30 miles NW, in heavy seas she broke clean in two amidships, her bow sinking, the remainder staying afloat long enough for the s.s *Vigilant* to rescue 15 crew, three having drowned.

8 February. *Tudor*, a sailing vessel which foundered off Scilly. March. *New Hampshire*. 'A chest and effects of Captain W. A. Lord, including money, two chronometers and clothing, were found amongst the rocks of Samson, which came from this vessel lost west of Scilly. The salvors behaved very honestly and well in the matter'

17 March. *Carnanton*, master Brabyn, a Welsh schooner carrying coal, was wrecked on Samson during an ESE gale. The sum of £8.9s.7d(£8.48) was given as remuneration to a boats crew of ten men who went to their assistance. The same day the Norwegian brig *Patrie*, master Hansen, from Odessa with linseed, foundered four miles NW of the Bishop after colli-

sion with the Norwegian barque *Vulcan*, two days earlier. Jacob Deason, pilot of St. Agnes went out in his cutter *Gem* and found her derelict seven miles south of St. Agnes, and she was later seen to founder a few miles NW of the Bishop Rock.

18 March. *Flink*, master Stawe, was seen offshore in distress, and the steamer *Little Western* took her in tow for two hours until she foundered four miles offshore. Crew saved.

23 March. *Noel Raphael*, master Bruneau, a brig of Nantes, Brest to Swansea in ballast, struck the Seven Stones and foundered.

June. *Thalia*, a Greek vessel, was put ashore on Queen's Ledge accidentally by a local pilot but suffered little damage. Fourteen men from St. Martin's stood by, who requested an award of £24, which, according to the Customs Officer was - 'a preposterous sum seeing the men did nothing'.

6 July. *David*, a brig bound for Newfoundland was sunk by collision with the s.s *Halley* at 7.30 a.m. 40 miles west of Scilly. Her eight man crew and three passengers were saved.

18 November. *Amelia*, a schooner carrying culm and four crew, foundered 13 miles east of the Bishop Rock.

December. *Good Intent*, a Portuguese brigantine with coal for Oporto, was lost at 1 a.m. in fog at the back of Great Ganilly.

1868 – 22 January. *Atlantic*, a local pilot cutter drove from her moorings in St. Mary's Pool, went on the rocks and was wrecked.

The Porthleven schooner *Brothers* was lost on the Seven Stones.

10 April. *Areta*, master Aveta, a Maltese ship in ballast, struck the Seven Stones knocking 20 feet of keel away, and entered Scilly for repairs with several feet of water in her hold.

May. *Gleaner*, master William Prance, a Newport brig carrying iron ore struck and sank on the Seven Stones. A writing desk, meat safe and letters were picked up off Land's End. Crew all lost.

20 August. *Logan*, master E. Gibson, of South Shields carrying coal, was seen to founder at 6 a.m. NE of the Seven Stones.

7 October. *Valiant*, a brig of Littlehampton on passage to Honfleur with coal, foundered in a gale 12 miles north of Scilly. One man lost.

21 November. *Caroline*, master Daventen, a French schooner laden with salt, drove on Mare Ledges at night and was lost. Crew saved.

22 November. *Margaret & Jane*, master John Stephens, a barque registered at Scilly, leaked so badly that when the *Inez* of Sunderland hove in sight, her officers and owner's son abandoned ship in a boat, leaving all the seamen on board, who were left to their fate. The derelict was picked up by the *Ezra*, towed into Scilly, condemned and broken up.

13 December. *Havelock*, master James Martin, of Chepstow, Tenema to Antwerp with zinc ore, was abandoned dismasted and sinking off Scilly. The local pilot-cutters *Presto* and *Atlantic* brought her to St. Mary's Pier, and were awarded £198 for the cargo, and £135 for saving the vessel.

14 December. *Quatre Freres et Marie*, a coal laden brigantine of Nantes, master Pouvreau, drove ashore on Tresco in a gale and became a total wreck. Crew saved.

1869 – 29 January. *Bertha*, master Burnard, a schooner of Bayonne carrying barley to Cardiff, in attempting to get into St. Martin's Bay during a WSW gale, struck on a ledge and sank. Crew saved.

30 January. *Huit Freres*, master Silo, a French brigantine loaded with coal for L'Orient, parted her cables at night in a gale and drove ashore on the SW side of Tresco where she became a wreck.

16 February. *Alida*, master Nagel, a Dutch schooner of Veendam, Swansea to Tarragonna with patent fuel, foundered three miles NE of White Island, her crew of eight men and a pilot being saved by the St. Martin's gig *Linnet*.

29 March. A vessel bottom up was found by a Scilly pilot-boat about three quarters of a mile south of the islands, drifting west with the tide. Her metal sheathing was very bright and clean, her rudder gone, and something dragging on the seabed brought her up on the Bishop Ridge, but by next morning she had disappeared.

31 August. *Oxus*, master John Dixon Wilson, a full-rigged ship of Dundee loaded with rice from Akyab which had called at Queenstown and been given orders for London. At 10.20 p.m. she struck the Pollard Rock, on the Seven Stones and sank. All 14 crew got into her gig and rowed for four and a half hours to reach the lightship.

4 December. *St. Lever*, master Brinquier, Antwerp to Swansea, saw a light between Land's End and Scilly, and supposing it was a ship tried to hail it, to say it was on the wrong tack, only to find the light was the Wolf Rock which this French vessel then struck! She got off fortunately with nothing worse than a damaged forefoot.

6 December. *Otto*, master Borjessen, a Swedish brigantine from Jacobstad to Bristol with tar, in bringing up in the Roads drove foul of the barque **Dorothy Thompson**, and went ashore on the SE corner of Samson and was lost. Some days later her captain almost drowned when he fell off the quay whilst seeing his crew off to Penzance! An interesting case of slander resulted in the Bodmin Court of Captain Peter Pender of Tresco and Frederick Hicks. By now Pender was the Postmaster, inn keeper and grocer on Tresco, and Hicks had accused him of stealing two cartloads of sails belonging to the wreck, despite the incident having taken place four years earlier. The defendants case was that a William Smith of Tresco stole the sails, removing them at midnight, and that Mr Augustus Smith must have been a participator. A verdict was returned for the defendant.

15 December. *Express*, a barque of Marseilles, Rio Congo to Caen with pistachio nuts parted both cables in a gale and went ashore at Porthloo and became a total wreck. Part of the cargo was saved.

30 December. *Ticina*, a French barque carrying oil nuts, drove ashore in a storm at Porthloo and was wrecked. At the same time the Waterford schooner *Margaret*, with pit wood, master Prendergast, drove ashore on Tean, between St. Martin's and Tresco, whilst the Prussian barque *Ida Maria* of and from Danzig went ashore at Carn Near filled, and had to have her deck cargo of timber unloaded before the *Little Western* steamer towed her off.

1870 – 11 January. *Petite Leocadie*, master le Boder, a French schooner carrying coal, put into Scilly on the 5th for repairs, and on completion was making her way from St. Mary's to New Grimsby without a pilot, when she struck on Rags Ledge and had to be run ashore. Her cargo was sold off at 15s.6d. a ton, and the complete vessel for £75.

27 January. *Willem Poelman*, a Dutch ship of and for Rotterdam from Batavia with sugar and coffee, dragged her anchors and went ashore on

Southern Wells near Samson. The steamer *Little Western* was lashed alongside, and using her pumps got her afloat, when two tugs towed her to Amsterdam. She left before a claim for £5,000 salvage award was settled for the *Little Western* and pilot-cutters.

2 April. *Sarah*. A Padstow schooner which struck the Bishop Rock, drifted off and foundered.

4 April. *St. Peterburg*, from Glasgow to Rotterdam, struck on a submerged rock on the edge of the Seven Stones and foundered.

20 April. *Sado*, master Robert Hoodless, a London steamer of 325 tons, Oporto to Liverpool carrying wool, wine, oranges, minerals, eggs and 30 head of cattle, struck the rocks in Smith's Sound at night in fog and sank. She went ashore on the Ledge of Rosevear. Her crew of 19, a stockman, the captain's wife and infant daughter and one passenger were all saved by boats from Scilly and a relief boat at the Bishop lighthouse. The wine was sold on St. Mary's between 4s.6d(22p) to16s(80p) per gallon depending on quality. 170 boxes of oranges fetched from 3s.9d(18p) to 6s.9d(33p) a box, whilst eggs were disposed of in lots of 8 dozen at 4d(2p) a dozen.

28 May. *Frances Jane*, master John Lavery, an Irish schooner carrying salt, when passing through St. Mary's Sound went ashore on Bartholemew Ledge at low water. She suffered considerable damage, her false keel floating away, and was brought into St. Mary's Pier for repairs. Her master thought he was in Whitesand Bay, passing between the Longships and Land's End!

21 July. *Tyne Queen*, master W. Loudon, a Liverpool steamer, went ashore on Man o'War Rock. Seven local gigs pulled her head around and with the aid of her sails the steamer reached St. Helen's Pool. Her bottom badly damaged but intact, a tug took her to Liverpool.

7 October. *Nelson*, a Fleetwood barque from Aguilas to the Tyne with 13 crew, struck the Seven Stones in fog and sank, taking her master and two seamen with her. The remaining crew reached the lightship, where they were stranded for three days until taken off by a Scilly pilot boat and landed at Penzance. She carried a cargo of lead and iron ore.

1871 – January. The brigantine *Royal Standard* was run on shore at Bryher having been on the rocks where she lost her keel but was got into

St. Mary's, and a Portuguese schooner was run on a beach on St. Mary's for safety. The **Royal Standard** was sold by auction for £50.

15 January. **Salmon**, master Jenkins, a brigantine of Scilly, owned by Captain James Phillips and Captain Deason, London to South Africa drove on to Mare Ledges. Several attempts to refloat her using steamships failed, and she was sold by auction on 09.02, to Joseph Denley of Penzance for £16.10s(£16.50). £390 was awarded the boatmen who saved her cargo of sweetmeats, candles, currants and sugar.

31 January. **E.R.I.** a Sunderland schooner of 121 tons net, from Montevideo to Falmouth with bone ash, hides and hooves, was wrecked at the back of White Island, St. Martin's during a gale. The crew landed using their own boat, some of the men walking into Higher Town before anyone knew of the wreck. Her remains were sold for 30 shillings (£1.50).

April. A Welsh schooner struck on Shipman Head, Bryher, but slipped off, drowning her crew, who had climbed on to her jib-boom.

24 June. **Primos**, of Bilbao, a barque of 406 tons, built in 1870, from Havana to Falmouth and then Greenock with sugar, struck the Seven Stones and sank in twelve minutes. The sole survivor, an Italian seaman named Vincenzo de Felice, was saved after swimming around for about two hours, then clinging to a floating hen coop for a further hour, then her figurehead for another hour after it became detached from the wreck, finally reaching the ship's boat which had capsized. Using one of her bottom boards, he then paddled towards St. Martin's Head, where fishermen picked him up. The figurehead is now in the Valhalla Collection.

7 July. **Belle of the South**, master Davis, from London to Algoa Bay with a general cargo, including earthenware, hams, glass, confectionery, corks, mace, ale, spirits and a large quantity of gun-powder in kegs. She struck Perconger Ledge, St. Agnes, and commenced to fill, reaching St. Mary's Quay with 8 feet of water in her hold. The agents, Messrs F. Banfield & Sons arranged that the entire quay was covered in sand, and that every fire in houses either side of the road leading up to the Garrison magazine was extinguished. Men were employed to carry the gunpowder kegs, each having been placed in a sack, on their backs to the magazine, where several tons were stored until the vessel was repaired.

20 October. **Due Fratelli**, of Naples, from Cronstadt, which had been

abandoned in the Bay of Biscay, was towed into Scilly derelict with nothing to show her name, nationality or destination. Her cargo of deals was discharged, and later her former name of *Salvatori* was found on her stern, under a piece of canvas, enabling her to be identified and claimed by a Mr Martini of Swansea as her owner.

20 December. *Delaware*, master Preston, a Liverpool steamship of 3,243 gross tons, carrying a general cargo, raw cotton and passengers from Liverpool to Calcutta sank between Seal Rock and Mincarlo. Her engine broke down and several men were badly injured, if not killed, before she got close to the shore where she foundered. Only 1st officer McWhinnie and 3rd officer Jenkins were saved. The men of Bryher carried the gig *Albion* from Great Par to Rushy Bay, then ten men used it to get to Sampson, again carrying the gig across the neck of the island to West Par, where she was launched into the teeth of a gale. Forty-seven men were lost when she went down on the Middle Ledges, and there is a story that her 1st officer prepared to defend himself on White Island against attack from the 'natives' by stoning his rescuers, having heard that they were little better than savages!

1872 – 13 February. *Ernst Von Homeyer*, a German barque from Hamburg to Buenos Ayres with a general cargo was found at sea derelict half full of water and badly damaged. The Scilly pilot cutter No 5, *Atlantic*, put out and brought her into St. Mary's. Her crew having landed at Dover, made their way to Penzance, reaching St. Mary's on the *Little Western*, and later manned her when a tug towed her to London.

17 February. *Telxinoi*. 'In the matter of the Greek brig stranded on the bar between St. Mary's and St. Martin's, the *Little Western* received by agreement £150 for her services. On Wednesday, the captain and crew of the pilot-cutter *Atlantic* summoned the captain of the brig before the magistrates for refusing to pay their claim of £80 for carrying off an anchor and chain, and mooring her in the Roads after being towed off by the steamship. The Court awarded them £24, the cutter's crew paying the costs, which reduced their award to £20.' In a letter to the editor of the Cornish Telegraph dated 06.03, Clement W. Mumford, Clerk to the Justices, St. Mary's, wrote 'It is entirely wrong that the costs were paid by

the cutter's crew; I have the award signed by the magistrates before me and it ends thus, " – we do hereby order and award that the said Captain Zafiropulo shall pay unto the said William Hicks and his crew £24 for their services aforesaid, together with £2.10s.6d(£2.52) costs and charges.'"

3 May. 'The fishing smack *Scud* of Lowestoft, which sank near Round Rock was raised, her starboard bilge much damaged.

9 June. The ship *John Phillips* of Glasgow, 368 tons gross, sprang a leak and foundered close to Scilly.

16 July. The Scilly/Penzance packet s.s *Earl of Arran,* of Penzance, 144 tons gross, master Deason, struck on a ledge when coming in through St. Martin's Neck and was run ashore on Nornour. She later broke in two amidships at low water and became a wreck. The crew and passengers were saved.

6 October. The Scilly/Penzance packet s.s *Little Western,* of Scilly, 115 tons gross, was wrecked on Southward Wells. She had been to the assistance of the French brigantine *Jane* which, however, was taken in tow by another steamer. It is said that Captain Hicks who commanded her was so angry at losing his salvage that he got drunk and ran the ship ashore. His son (or possibly his nephew) afterwards became Bishop of Lincoln.

22/23 November. The Italian barque *Rosa Tacchini*, master Abbate (or Abbati), from Buenos Aires for Antwerp with hides, tallow and wool, parted one of cables in St. Mary's Road during a heavy south-westerly gale at night. She struck on Paper Ledge and eventually went to pieces off Carn Near.

1873 – *Fanny* was wrecked on the Seven Stones.

1 February. The chasse maree *Jeune Austerlitz* of Andrey, master Le Moulin, from Cardiff for Brest with coal, ran on Crow Bar at low water during a strong south-easterly gale. The crew were saved. No pilot was on board.

3 February. A large black brigantine of Llanelly, with new double topsails, apparently outward bound, was seen to strike on the Seven Stones at noon. She foundered half an hour later close to the French schooner *Aimable Jeanne* which was unable to render assistance and it was supposed that all the crew were lost.

15/16 March. *Elizabeth* was lost with all hands. Much of the wreckage was washed up on St. Agnes.

9 June. The fishing lugger *Cornish Girl* of Penzance, 16 tons net, struck on Round Rock, between the Spanish Ledges and the Gugh, and foundered in deep water. The crew were taken off by another lugger. (According to one account she was *Cornish Lass* of Mousehole, and was wrecked on the 7th June 1874).

December. An unidentified ship foundered on the Seven Stones.

1874 – *Charles Eugene* was lost on the Seven Stones.

January. A British steamer foundered west of Scilly.

18 January. The ship *Minnehaha*, 845 tons net, master Jones, from Callao via Falmouth for Dublin with guano, was wrecked between Peninnis Outer Head and Pulpit Rock in thick weather. The master, pilot, and eight of the crew were drowned but the mate and eight or nine others took refuge in the tops from where they dropped down the bowsprit stays onto the rocks of the headland.

22 March. *James Armstrong*, a derelict with cargo of mahogany, was towed into Crow Sound by pilot boats and subsequently into St. Mary's Harbour, where she was repaired before being towed away. It was later discovered that she had struck somewhere on the Irish coast and drifted off, then on the Seven Stones and drifted clear again. All hands were lost.

4 April. The s.s *Bordelaise* of Liverpool, 691 tons gross, master O'Keefe, from Newport for Oporto with coal and railway iron, was wrecked on the Hats.

13 April. The pilot cutter *Gem* of Scilly, 30 tons, broke adrift from her moorings during a gale and was wrecked. Her destruction was a great loss to her crew as she was their sole means of livelihood.

13 April. the brigantine *Tonkin*, master Gyles, from Cardiff for Dakar with coal, foundered off Scilly.

16 April. s.s *Zelda,* of Liverpool, 1,411 tons gross, master Pierce, from Liverpool for Palermo with general cargo, struck on Maiden Bower, in a dense fog, shortly after midnight and sank. The crew of thirty-two and her passengers were saved and much of the cargo afterwards salved by divers. She was less than thirty-two hours out of Liverpool on her maiden voyage.

16 April. The brig *Triron* of Cardigan, with coal, foundered near the Western Rocks.

1875 – The *Ann* was wrecked, and the *Ville de Rocheller* was lost on the Seven Stones.
14 February. The barque *Floresta* of Sunderland, 299 tons net, master White, from Taganrog via Falmouth for Cork with wheat having called at Falmouth for orders, struck on the Seven Stones during a dense fog and sank almost immediately. The crew were picked up by the French lugger *Josephine*.
7 May. The German mail-steamer *Schiller*, at that time one of the largest vessels afloat, foundered on the Retarrier Ledges with the loss of 335 lives. Only thirty-six men and one woman were saved. *Schiller* was an iron screw steamer built in Glasgow in 1873 by Napier and Sons. She was 3,421 tons gross, 380 feet long, 40 feet beam and 24 feet depth of hold. She belonged to the German Transatlantic Steam Navigation Co. of Hamburg, which, amalgamated with the Eagle Line, was one of the biggest lines in existence. She was bound from New York for Plymouth, Cherburg and Hamburg and carried 300,000 dollars specie for Cherburg and the British mails from New Zealand. She carried 372 people in all, mostly Germans, of whom 254 were passengers. On the night of the wreck, and when ahead of schedule, she ran into thick fog. In fifteen minutes it was impossible to see the length of the ship. Sail was at once taken in, the engines reduced to half speed and the lookout was increased, but, because of the density of the fog and the impossibility of seeing anything or of hearing the fog bell from the lighthouse, *Schiller* had come inside the Bishop by half a mile. At 22.00 hrs. the ship struck with a violent crash. The fog, the heavy sea, the darkness, the slippery decks, and the angle at which the ship lay, all combined to magnify the horror of the catastrophe. Seven of the eight boats were got out, but only three were successfully launched and one of these capsized. A signal gun was fired some half a dozen times and, when the powder became wet, rockets were sent up but failed to bring assistance, only one signal gun being heard on St. Mary's. This was assumed to be a signal that the *Schiller* had passed the Bishop, and was reported to the agent at Plymouth as the usual report gun.

At 2 a.m. the captain, doctor and chief engineer were washed overboard. Shortly afterwards the deck 'pavillion' or round-house in which practically all the women and children had taken refuge was washed away, one of her iron masts following it.

At daybreak two boats came out from St. Agnes, one owned by Obadiah Hicks, but could pick up only seven men swimming in the sea, it being impossible to approach the wreck. A message was sent to St. Mary's for the steam packet *Lady of the Isles* and the lifeboat, but on reaching the wreck found the last mast had fallen, carrying with it many survivors, and they were only able to pick up bodies and 23 mail bags. The two remaining lifeboats reached Tresco landing 27 survivors. Divers recovered £50,000 in specie, and 2,399 $20 gold pieces. Accounts vary as to the total number of passengers and crew carried, also how many survived.

10 July. *Hound*, a six-oared gig returning to St. Mary's after a cricket match on Tresco sank, and four men, W. P. Hicks, Walter Hicks, Walter Legg and Sanderson Phillips all drowned.

2 November. *Catherine Griffiths*, master Henry Jones, a Sunderland brig for Rio de Janeiro with coal, struck Gorregan at night in fog and was lost with only one survivor.

2 November. *Aksai*, master Boltine, a Russian steamship from Cardiff to Odessa with coal, went ashore on White Island, St. Martin's at 2 a.m. in fog. Her crew of 40 were landed on St. Mary's by the *Lady of the Isles*, the vessel becoming a total wreck.

23 November. *Foscolo*, master Costa, an Italian barque from Monte Video for Dundee with bones and scrap iron, struck on the Seven Stones at 2 p.m, got off, but two hours later was run ashore on Crow Bar and saved.

1876 – 9 March. *Linn Fern*, a ship from Glasgow, was wrecked on Crow Bar.

August. *Elaine*, a yacht which filled in heavy seas and sank in St. Mary's Roads. Her crew of two were saved by a French brig.

1877 – 24 January. *Essie*, master R. Farquar, a Banff schooner of 99 tons was seen on fire and apparently abandoned ten miles south of St. Agnes. During the afternoon pilot cutters went out to her but were too late to be of any assistance. She is believed to have carried coal, tar and pitch and sank some 20 miles S x E. of Scilly.

29 April. *Hendon*, master R. Doughty, a Sunderland brig carrying salt from Liverpool to Kronstadt. Having developed a leak, her pumps choked, and when ten miles NNE of Scilly her crew were taken off by the French schooner *Jeune Henri*. The brig foundered shortly after she had been abandoned.

10 October. *William van Name*, master Coggins, an American barque on passage from New York to Cork with grain, struck the Seven Stones at 5.30 a.m. Her crew took to the boats and reached the lightship, but later returned to their ship, but she went down at 6.40 a.m. without loss of life.

1878 – 29 March. *Frederick*, a schooner of Llanelly, which was in collision with the brig *Meenstadt* of Norway, off Scilly during a snow squall. Two men were saved but the master, his two sons and the mate's wife were all lost.

9 April. *Surprise*, a derelict French schooner of Vannes, laden with pitwood was towed into St. Mary's. 'Mr. John Banfield jnr, vice-consul for France, called upon the Customs Officer and produced authority to claim her, and after payment of all expenses and giving Bond to secure the salvors, I gave the said vessel up to him.'

31 December. *Minerve* (or *Minerva*), master Bodiquet, of St. Malo, Swansea to Cadiz with coal, drove ashore on Morning Point and was wrecked. The gig *Hope* saved one man, five others being rescued by breeches buoy.

1879 – January. *Gellert*, a sailing vessel was lost in collision with the *Rozella Smith*; the *Marie Victorina* sank following collision with an unidentified vessel, and the crew of the brig *Maggie*, of Llanelly were rescued by the St. Martin's pilot-cutter *Argus*, having presumably foundered.

23 January. *Bertha*, master Williams, a Liverpool barque carrying guano from Peru to Antwerp, was in collision with the American ship *T. H. Brown* who saved her 16 man crew. The Scilly pilot-cutter *Agnes* found the abandoned vessel with three masts and her bowsprit gone, but managed to save the chronometer, two sextants and a barometer, leaving her

with the upper deck completely awash.

26 February. *Rosaire*, master Francois Biron, a French brig carrying coal from Newport to Brest, struck submerged wreckage near the Seven Stones, and her crew barely had time to prepare one boat before she went down, drowning three men. Four survivors were picked up by the *Queen*, of Scilly, and landed on St. Mary's.

24 March. *Tobasco*, master Jean Jules Dusson, a Bordeaux barquentine, carrying coal and bottled beer from Greenock, drove ashore on White Island, St. Martin's. She was only two weeks into her maiden voyage, her master having mistaken the Seven Stones light for Trevose Head. The wreck was sold for £1.10s (£1.50), the 80 ton coal cargo £2 and the beer for 4s.6d.(23p).

27 July. *Maipu*, master Thomas Wheeler, a Liverpool barque of 594 tons, Iquique to Hamburg with saltpetre, drove ashore in Hell Bay at night in fog and was lost. Her stern board is in the Valhalla Collection. The wreck was sold for £7, but 16 days later went to pieces and no cargo was saved.

27 July. *River Lune*, master George West, a Liverpool barque of 1,172-tons, L'Orient to Ardrossan in ballast, was lost on Isinvrank (a rock in Muncoy Neck, near Melledgan) at night, in fog. Her crew of 20 took to two boats and landed next morning at St. Agnes. Her figure-head in is the Valhalla Collection.

30 October. *St. Jacques*, master Legoff, a French sloop of Hornfleur, Le Havre to Swansea in ballast, ran aground at the back of Brhyer having lost her mainsail and her pumps becoming choked.

1880 – *Queen*, a 24-ton pilot cutter of St. Martin's, is said to have gone ashore on Par Beach, St. Martin's and became a total loss.

A ship's name board bearing the name *Voltri* in gilt lettering on a blue background was found ashore at the back of St. Mary's, and was believed to be from the barque *Voltri* of Genoa, 578-tons.

28 April. *Chard*, of Bridgwater, with slates, foundered off Scilly after being dismasted. The crew were saved by a Norwegian barque and were landed at Scilly by the pilot cutter *Atlantic*.

9 October. *Strathisla*, master John Dimond, of Exeter, 71-tons. 'The Scilly Magistrates awarded £48 to the gig *Bernice*, and the pilot-cut-

ters *Atlantic* and *Presto* for towing into port on the 10th the derelict *Strathisla*, Port Talbot to Plymouth with coal. £15 has also been awarded to the pilot cutter *Agnes* for picking up the crew.'

23 October. *Flossie*, master J. Robin, a Guernsey brig of 174-tons in ballast for Swansea, was abandoned due to a severe leak 25 miles north of Scilly and left on her beam-ends. On the same day, the schooner *Argo*, master Lewis, of Dublin, from Newport to Polruan with coal, leaked 30 miles W of Lundy in a gale and ran for Scilly. She struck a ledge near Tean and was wrecked, crew saved.

28 October. *Messenger*, master Thomas Penrose Skenleberry, a Salcombe brig of 193-tons, carrying coal to Portsmouth, anchored in St. Mary's Roads, parted, and drove ashore on Skirt Island, Tresco. Her crew were saved by the lifeboat. The wreck was sold to Messrs F. Banfield and was broken up on St. Mary's.

31 October. The Coastguard on St. Martin's picked up wreckage from the *Five Sisters*, of Goole, master Thomas Lowther.

1881 – 5 January. *St. Jean*, a Bordeaux barque of 589-tons and 16 crew and one passenger, collided with the barque *Privateer* six miles SW of Wolf Rock and sank with the loss of three lives.

18 January. *Charlotte Dunbar*, master Guillon, a brigantine of L'Orient, 82-tons, coal laden, was wrecked at night in a snow storm on Burnt Island, St. Agnes. She became a total wreck and her five crew were supposed lost.

4 March. *Bangalore*, master J. Roberts, a barque of Greenock, 398-tons carrying coal, eleven crew and a stowaway. Heavy seas carried away her deck-house and partly flooded her hold. After pumping all day the crew refused to work any longer and she was abandoned to sink 25 miles north of Scilly.

7 May. *Culmore*, master A. Coble, a steamship of 540-tons, from Valencia to Liverpool with oranges, pepper and onions, struck the Crim at night in dense fog and foundered. Eighteen crew saved themselves in their own boats, but the captain, 1st & 2nd engineers and a steward drowned.

24 September. *Indipendenza*, master F. Cafferina, an Italian barque of Genoa, 795-tons, Valparasio via Bristol for Rotterdam with hides, horns

and guano, struck heavily on the Western Rocks in fog. She got off but then struck the Crim where she ramained for 4 minutes before floating off. Her crew of 14 and a Channel pilot, took to the boats and followed the abandoned vessel all the way to the Barrel of Butter, St. Mary's, where she drove ashore and was wrecked.

21 November. **Gem**, master George Gibson, a double-ended paddle steamer of Liverpool, 118-tons, from Holyhead for the Brass River in West Africa, parted her cables and drove ashore at Porthloo and became a wreck. Her crew of 14 were all saved.

27 November. **Excelsior**, master R. Loose, a German barque of Hamburg, 640-tons, from Rangoon for Scilly for orders, carrying rice, teak and rattans, parted her cables in the Roads during a westerly gale and heavy seas. Gigs from Bryher and St. Mary's reached the barque who went on board to assist the crew. A jib was hoisted with the intention of running for Falmouth, but she struck Crow Bar, leaked, and had to be beached on St. Martin's. Her cargo was saved and she was refloated, but whilst being towed for St. Mary's on 22.01.1882 capsized on top of the s.s **Queen of the Bay**, carrying away the steamer's mainmast, and sank, nearly drowning some 50 islanders who were on board. She was later broken up.

1882 – 30 January. **Richard Warbrick** of Fleetwood, master J. Osborne, 107-tons, from Runcorn with coal, stranded on the Seven Stones and became a wreck, only one man being saved.

24 April. **St. Vincent**, master G. Melhuish, of London, 479-tons, from St. Vincent to Scilly for orders with sugar and cotton, struck the Spanish Ledges and later foundered while at anchor off Toll's Island. Her crew of 17 saved themselves in their own boats.

13 November. **Eliza**, master William Lurn, a Jersey brig, 211-tons, Swansea to Honfleur with coal, put into Scilly leaking badly and ran aground near St. Martin's Head. She later reached St. Mary's.

1883 – 26 January. **Arzilla**. A ship's board bearing this name together with a boat rudder and deck planking was picked up on Samson and St. Mary's, and she was believed lost with 30 crew.

9 February. **Criccieth Castle**, master James Morris, a brig of Portmadoc,

218-tons, Fray Bentos via Falmouth for Liverpool with guano, struck Peninnis at night in a gale and sank. All six crew and a Falmouth pilot drowned, and Porthcressa was covered in wreckage.

6 June. *Ala Charles*, master Richard Edwards, an Aberystwyth schooner, 74-tons, carrying 125 tons of bar iron sank 4 miles SE of the Seven Stones lightship after her cargo broke through her side.

1884 – 13 February. *Moel Rhiwan*, master J. Williams, an iron barque of Carnarvon, 1086-tons carrying coal for Valparaiso, foundered off Scilly in a heavy gale. Her crew were saved.

13 September. 'At 11 a.m. a large barque off the Seven Stones, steering ESE, was seen to suddenly disappear. A gun was fired from the lightship, and no doubt she was from Queenstown, and presume she sank after striking the Stones. Wind ENE, light & hazy.

1885 – 8 June. *Earl of Lonsdale*, master L. Davis, a Newcastle steamer of 1,543-tons, Alexandria to Portishead with beans and cotton seed, went ashore in fog near Troy Town, St. Agnes, and became a wreck. Her crew of 22 were all saved.

17 December. *Sussex*, master R. M. Robinson, a London steamer, 2,795-tons, Baltimore to London with a general cargo and 250 head of cattle, drove ashore on Seal Rock at 2 a.m. in fog. Her crew of 45 were saved and 24 bullocks were landed on Gweal. Flour, tin food lard and leather were saved before she became a total wreck.

30 December. *Plump*, master J. Jenkins, a 2-ton cutter, capsized off Yellow Ledge on her way to the wreck of the *Sussex*. W. Hicks, the other crew member, drowned.

1886 – 26 March. *Nellie*, master M. Svendsen, a Danish brigantine of Elisnore, 315-tons, Bordeaux to Cardiff with pit props, was lost on the Brow of the Ponds, near Rosevear. Her 2nd mate and four seamen landed on Melledgan after three hours on a raft, the vessel having gone to pieces. The master and chief officer drowned.

1887 – 12 January. *Bolina*, master J. Willoughby, a Carnarvon schooner of 98-ton, Portmadog to London with 180 tons of slates, missed stays when entering St. Mary's Sound during a gale at night and was wrecked on the Gugh. Her crew of five were saved.

8 June. *Castleford*, master L. McLean, a Liverpool steamship of 3,044-tons, Montreal to London with a general cargo and 450 head of cattle, ran ashore in fog at night on Crebawethan. Her crew were saved and most of the cattle landed on Annet.

9 July. *Barremann*, master Law, an iron barque of Glasgow, for San Fransisco, with coke, bricks, cement and pig iron, was lost on the Seven Stones with all hands. The fishing boat *Louisa* of Mousehole, discovered one of her topmasts standing two feet above the waves.

12 December. *Brighouse*, master T. Tregarthen, a Cardiff steamship of 952-tons, from Bordeaux with pit props, was lost in fog on the Seven Stones. Her 15 crew reached the lightship in two boats.

1888 – 15 January. *Gauloise*, master Raoul Harand, a Bordeaux barque of 332-tons, for Porthcawl with pit props, was lost in fog on Lady Ledge, between Ragged Island and Little Arthur. All 11 crew were saved, and her figurehead is now in the Valhalla Collection.

11 March. *Benardo*, master Andrea Dapelo a Genoese barque of 701-tons, Alicante to Cardiff in ballast, was wrecked at the back of Annet. All 12 crew took to their boat which capsized, drowning the occupants except the master who was rescued by the St. Agnes gig *O. & M*. The Valhalla Collection has her figurehead.

25 April. *Cubana*, a Sunderland barque, Swansea to Cuba with coal, iron and mining equipment, was lost on the Seven Stones. Her master and six crew were lost, but the mate, nine seamen and a passenger rowed the ship's boat to the lightship.

9 August. *Gomes V*, master Antonio d'Azevedo, a steamship of Lisbon, 736-tons, Cardiff to Oporto with coal, was wrecked in the Eastern Isles on Shag Rock. Her 18 crew landed on St. Mary's.

1889 – 3 March. *Jane Owen*, master Richard Jenkins, a Carnarvon schooner, 76-tons, Aberdovey to Plymouth with 130 tons of slates, dragged her anchor in New Grimsby Channel and was lost on the Half-Tide Rock. Her four man crew landed on Tresco having saved only their clothes when the ship fell over. As with so many other wrecks, her figure-head was added to the Valhalla Collection.

September. **Felix Guemole**, an Italian brigantine, was wrecked in heavy seas, crew saved.

1890 – The name board of a Portuguese vessel **Corea**, was picked up on Scilly, and donated to Valhalla, giving rise to the assumption she was lost at sea somewhere off the islands. At the same time, an unidentified French steamship was believed to have been lost with all hands on the Seven Stones.

25 May. **Albana**, master C. Murray, a Sunderland iron steamship, 1,522-tons, Baltimore to Rotterdam with a general cargo, sank following collision with the s.s **Nerissa** 30 miles SW of the Wolf Rock. Of her 26 crew, only one man was lost.

30 December. **Marie Eugenie**, a barque of Nantes, Le Havre for Newport in ballast, was running for St. Mary's without a pilot when she drove ashore on Great Ganilly bar where she was damaged. She was later brought into St. Mary's Roads.

1891 – 5 February. **Chiswick**, master W. Hughes, a London steamer of 1,262-tons, Cardiff to St. Nazaire with coal, struck the Pollard Rock, Seven Stones and sank. Whilst preparing the boats, the ship lurched to starboard and disappeared underwater, carrying with her everything except the port lifeboat which floated clear but then capsized, leaving her 2nd mate and seven men clinging to the keel. Seaman Thomas Hole used his initiative by saving a boathook, to which he attached his handkerchief, and used it as a distress signal, without which the crew of the lightship, some 3 miles distant would never have seen them after the steamship sank.

9 March. **Eliza**, a Bideford smack, carrying salt from Gloucester to Penzance with a crew of three, was wrecked amongst the Western Rocks, during the Great Blizzard. A major part of the vessel found ashore at Melledgan was identified by a blue stocking marked 'JW' on a corpse which proved to be that of her mate, James Wood. During the same easterly hurricane and heavy snow, the Plymouth trawler **Mary Jane** was

found on the rocks of Scilly on 16.03 and the smack **Porth** of Padstow, master J. Billing, carrying 60 tons of culm from Swansea to Penzance. Her master and his son were rescued by the St. Agnes lifeboat **James & Caroline**, her mate having drowned. At the same time the 78-ton schooner **Martha**, sank 4 miles NE of the Wolf Rock carrying slates; the ketch **Alberta** was lost following collision off the Seven Stones, and on 12.03 the Dutch barque **Megellan**, 500-tons, master Schapp, was abandoned sinking off the Bishop, whilst the **Frere et Soeur** went to pieces on Pelistry Ledge. Her crew of five jumped overboard to swim for the shore, but only the master and the mate reached the beach alive.

13 March. **Roxburgh Castle**, a Newcastle steamer, Newport to Pireaus with coal, sank following collision with the **British Peer** SW of the Scillies and sank with 22 crew, only two men being saved.

11 November. **J. K. A.**, master William Escott, a Padstow schooner of 60-tons, Ballinacurra to Poole with oats, was lost on Shag Rocks. Her crew reached Great Innisvouls, from where they were rescued by a gig and landed at St. Martin's. The wreck drifted off and sank.

1892 – 6 February. **Embiricos**, master J. Lukisias, a Greek steamer, Cardiff to Malta with coal, struck rocks off the back of St. Martin's at 4.30 a.m. in fog and sank in deep water. Twelve crew and three Maltese passengers landed on St. Martin's, but her captain, mate, bosun, four engineers and three other passengers all drowned.

29 February. **Plato**, a Liverpool steamer of 1,675-tons, on passage to South America with a general cargo, sank off Scilly when her propeller shaft broke and went through the ship's side. Her 29 crew were all saved, picked up by the s.s **J. W. Taylor**.

1 October. **Camiola**, master W. Story, a Newcastle steamer, of 2,226-tons, Barry to Malta with coal, foundered a few minutes after striking the Seven Stones. All 24 crew were saved.

1893 – 10 March. **Le Bearnais**, master F. Finkernagel, a French barque of 388-tons, Le Havre to Cardiff in ballast, sank six miles W of the Bishop following collision with the s.s **Llanberis**. All saved.

4 April. **Horsa**, master J. Robson, an iron full-rigged ship of Liverpool,

1,163-tons, Bluff Harbour, New Zealand, for Scilly for orders, carrying oats, tinned meat, wool and three passengers stranded in Bread & Cheese Cove, St. Martin's. Towed off by the s.s *Lyonnesse* and leaking badly, she sank 20 miles SW of Scilly.

24 November. *Serica*, master Sydney Smith, a London steamship, 2,652-tons, Cardiff to Port Said with coal came into the Roads with storm damage and heavy list, her captain having been swept overboard twice and both times been washed back again. After repairs at St. Mary's, she sailed without a pilot, but struck a then uncharted rock off the Garrison, now named Serica Rock and sank. Her figurehead is now displayed in the Valhalla Collection.

1894 – Early January. *Afon Cefni*. The Custom's Officer on Scilly wrote to the owner of this vessel, a Charles Pierce, of Bangor, on 01.02, to say that a piece of wood, apparently part of a ship's rail, marked *Afon Cefni*, and a lifebuoy marked with the same name and flags had been picked up on Scilly, suggesting she was lost.

1895 – Wreckage of a French chasse maree fishing boat was found washed up in Gimble Porth, with no trace of her crew.

17 February. *Sultana*, a Swedish barque was abandoned off the Bishop after developing a leak and foundered. Crew saved.

1896 – 20 August. *Havire la Monette*, master Botrel, a French schooner of 133-tons, sank off Scilly following collision.

21 August. *Kong Sverre*, master T. Petersen, a Norwegian barque of 540-tons, carrying coal from Cardiff to Kingston, was lost amongst the Western Rocks at night.

29 November. *Ocean Belle*, master B. Hughes, a Beaumaris schooner, of 62-tons, for London with slates, after being dismasted drifted to within three miles of Scilly, when the St. Agnes lifeboat went out and took off her three man crew, leaving her to founder.

15 December. *Sophie*, master C. Bjorge, a Norwegian barque, 554-tons was seen dismasted three miles north of the Shipman Head, and both a Bryher boat and the s.s *Lady of the Isles* left to assist. The only life on

The Cypriot motor vessel *Poleire* on Little Kettle Rock, in Tresco Sound, laden with zinc-ore, after going ashore on 15 April 1970.

Acknowledgment: Frank Gibson

board was a dog, and the vessel was towed in by the mail steamer. Her owners attempted to claim the vessel through the dog, but she was sold with her cargo of anthracite to Dorrien Smith of Tresco for £250, who had her beached at New Grimsby and broken up.

1897 – A disabled schooner carrying codfish was sighted offshore, and a lifeboat and a gig put off and found her almost awash. The s.s *Lyonnesse* took her in tow, but she sank in Broad Sound.

5 April. *Palmos*, a 3-masted Norwegian schooner, Cardiff to Para with coal, was abandoned 10 miles NW of the Bishop. The Falmouth tugs *Eagle* and *Dragon* were sent, but she foundered soon after.

5 July. *Heathmore*, master A. F. Hird, Bilbao to Glasgow with iron ore, struck the Seven Stones and sank in deep water some hours later. Nineteen crew all saved and landed at Penzance.

1898 – 25 January. *Craig Elvan*, master H. M. Saunders, a barque of Greenock, 1,412-tons gross, Iquique to Ghent with nitrate of soda. Struck on the Crebinicks at 5 a.m. in dense fog and foundered shortly after having opened up several hull plates. Her crew of 22 got away in their boats, and were guided to St. Mary's by gigs from St. Agnes.

26 May. *Nyanza*, master Alfred Richards, a Newlyn fishing lugger, struck on the Crim, and having no punt on board, ran her ashore on Crebawethan. Her crew of six, with all their effects were taken off and landed, the vessel abandoned as a total loss.

20 August. *Toledo*, master J. Wishart, a steamship from Galveston to Rotterdam with a general cargo of about 4,500-tons which included wheat and oil cake, struck a rock in the North Channel, probably Steeple Rock, in dense fog, and sank in ten minutes. Her crew of 28 took to a lifeboat and a gig, and had barely cleared the vessel when her stern lifted high in the air and she sank by the head. The wreck was blown up by divers, it being a hazard to shipping.

15 December. *Brinkburn*, master James Martin, a London registered steamship of 3,229-tons gross, from Galveston to Le Havre with a crew of 39 and a cargo of cotton and cotton seed. Whilst proceeding in dense fog

at 2.5 knots, she stranded on Maiden Bower at 11.45 p.m. Her crew landed on Bryher from their own boats, but the vessel became a total loss,
breaking in two. On 24.12 the s.s *Hyaena* of Liverpool arrived in Scilly to
commence saving the 9,000 bales of cotton on board worth £100,000.

1899 – An unidentified steamship flying French colours, was seen to
founder off the Seven Stones. Nothing of her or her crew is known.
12 February. *Bohallard*, master and owner J. Noblanc, a French brigantine of Nantes, 76-tons net, carrying coal from Newport to Audierne. She
parted both cables in a gale and ran ashore on St. Mary's, floated off to
drift ashore on an island near St. Martin's. The rocket apparatus went to
the scene, but the crew walked ashore at low tide.
9 April. *Allington*, a Norfolk ketch carrying 4,000 sets of boxwood, from
Fenit, in Ireland, was seen abandoned three miles from St. Martin's Head.
James Nance and 12 other Scillonian boatmen put out in a gig, boarded
her, pumped her out and brought her in to St. Mary's derelict, where she
was handed to the Receiver of Wreck. She had been abandoned off the
Longships, and her crew, apart from one man who drowned, landed at
Dover from the s.s *Maidstone*.
25 October. *Erik Rickmers*, master H. Verthmann, a full-rigged ship of
Bremerhaven, 130 days out from Bangkok for Bremen with rice, struck
Scilly Rock in dense fog at 9 p.m. Her crew of 26 stood by the ship for
four hours in their boats, before being guided to Bryher by pilots. The
vessel sank at 2 a.m. next day in deep water.
26 October. *Parame*, master Jeauno, a French barque of 364-tons gross,
carrying coconuts from Trinidad to London, also struck Scilly Rock and
went ashore only 150 yards away from the *Erik Rickmers*. Both ships had
sailed in company all the previous day, and were wrecked within a few
hours of each other. Bryher boats rescued all ten of her crew.

1900 – 13 May. *Star*, master Mann, a ketch of Scilly, owned by John
Banfield, carrying coal from Wales, stranded on Bacon Ledge at night
whilst entering port. She floated off at 2 a.m. and went alongside the quay
at St. Mary's for examination.

1901 – 22 June. *Falkland*, master George Gracie, a Liverpool barque of 2,676-tons net, from Tacoma to Falmouth for orders, with wheat, a crew of 31 and two passengers, struck the Bishop Rock in fog, after twice missing stays. Her mainyard actually struck the Bishop Rock lighthouse and she sank nearby. Her captain and five crew drowned; the survivors, which included the captain's wife and child, were landed by the St. Agnes lifeboat *James & Caroline*. The figurehead of the *Falkland* is in the Valhalla Collection.

1902 – 2 February. *Lafaro*, an Italian barque of Naples, 721-tons gross, Hamburg to Cardiff in ballast, was seen to capsize north of St. Martin's Head at 5 p.m. in an easterly gale and heavy seas, and is believed to have been driven on the Merrick rocks. She broke up and all her crew drowned, the St. Mary's lifeboat having found no survivors. The St. Martin's gig *Emperor* put out with 14 men, but the rescue attempt was abandoned due to heavy seas. Her figurehead is also in the Valhalla Collection.
5 July. *Reginald*, master Kent, a Plymouth registered steam trawler, went ashore at Porth Hellick, but was towed off by the Falmouth tug *Eagle*, having received only slight damage forward.

1903 – 25 May. *Loretio*. A Peruvian river gunboat, captain Baker, recently built at Birkenhead, and being delivered to Peru with a crew of 14, foundered off Scilly at night, her crew being landed at Plymouth next day by the French trawler *Charlotte*.
28 July. *Ruperra*, master J. Pengelly, a Cory Line collier of Cardiff, 2,792-tons net, on passage from Barry to Port Said, was run down and sunk by HM cruiser *Melampus* at night 15 miles SW of Scilly.
20 September. *Queen Mab*, master Henry Boxall, a Glasgow barque, Punta Arenas to Falmouth with fustic (a yellow dye wood), struck Spanish Ledges. Leaking badly she anchored, but after slipping her cables was towed in by the s.s *Lyonesse* and beached in a sinking condition. Claims for salvage compensation were made in the High Court by the West Cornwall S.S Co, owners of the *Lyonesse*; the crew of the St. Mary's lifeboat *Henry Dundas*, the St. Agnes lifeboat *James & Caroline*, and owners and crew of the gigs *Lee* and *O & M*. The defendants admitted the

services, but claimed the plaintiff's amount was exaggerated. The value of property saved was £8,299. The *Lyonesse* was awarded £1,250, the *Henry Dundas* and *Lee* £225 between them; the *O & M* £150, and the *James & Caroline* £75, a total award of £1,700.

1904 – January. *Famiglia Cavallo*, a Genoese barque, 820-tons gross, was lost off Scilly after being abandoned.
13 July. *Phosphor*, a Liverpool steamship of 2,071-tons gross, carrying gasoline in drums from Middlesbrough to Braila. She was involved in collision whilst under tow off Scilly and foundered.
13 August. HMS *Decoy*, Lieut. W. D. Paton, RN, a torpedo-boat destroyer, was sunk following collision with HMS *Arun* between the Wolf Rock and Isles of Scilly at night. One man was lost.

1905 – January. *Carapanama*, master Wheelam, a Brazilian steamship, foundered 20 miles NE of Bishop Rock in a gale with all 12 crew, some time between the 1st & 5th January.
10 March. *Viking*, master J. Barber, a 1-ton cutter yacht, registered at Scilly, sailing from Bryher to St. Mary's, struck Bacon Ledge and foundered, her master and owner being drowned.
15 June. *Hydrangea*, master J. Taylor, a Milford steam trawler of 145-tons gross, struck the Seven Stones at 10.30 p.m. and sank. Her crew of nine and a dog left in their leaking punt, which was in danger of sinking, when a boat from the Seven Stones lightship reached them as the punt went down.

1906 – 3 June. *Magdeleine*, master Nicholas Gence, a Boulogne registered, iron steam trawler of 208-tons gross. She came in on the Sunday evening to land an injured crewman who needed to see a doctor, passing over Bartholomew Ledges the wrong side of the buoy at high water. She sailed the same day at 7.30 p.m, but at low tide struck the ledges and sank within ten minutes, a total loss.
5 June. *General Roberts*, master John Pettit, a steam trawler of Hull, with a crew of nine, which developed a severe leak in the engine-room and sank 12 miles NE of Round Island, going down in 40 fathoms, her crew

landing on Tresco after rowing for seven hours.

22 July. *King Cadwallon*, master George Mowat, a Glasgow steamship of 3,275-tons gross, Barry to Naples with 5,043 tons of coal and a crew of 27, struck Hard Lewis in fog and became a total loss. Her crew escaped in their own boats and reached St. Mary's.

1907 – 16 October. *St. Christophe*, master K. Alexandre, a French crab-bing cutter, stranded on Innisidgen and became a total loss. Her crew of five were saved.

14 December. *Thomas W. Lawson*, master George Dow, a 5,218-tons gross, seven-masted steel schooner, one of the largest sailing ships ever built, carrying 2,225,000 gallons of kerosene in cans, mistook the Bishop Rock lighthouse for a passing ship in bad visibility, and on 13.12 found herself inside the Crim. Unable to alter course and in great danger, two anchors were dropped in the hope she could ride out the storm. The keep-ers on the Bishop Rock fired distress signals at 4 p.m, which brought out both the St. Agnes and St. Mary's lifeboats. Captain Dow was urged to abandon ship, but replied he had ridden out worse storms and had confi-dence in his anchors and chain. The St. Agnes lifeboat coxswain replied, 'Beg your pardon, but you are not alright. You may have ridden out storms on the other side of the Atlantic Ocean, but not where you are now!' The captain did however, ask for a pilot, and William Thomas Hicks (known as Billy Cook) went on board. In heavy seas, the St. Mary's lifeboat broke her mast against the schooner's stern and put back to St. Mary's for repairs and to request tugs from Falmouth. Later that evening, whilst the St. Agnes lifeboat lay astern of the schooner, one of the lifeboat crew named William Francis Hicks was found unconscious in the bottom of the boat and obviously ill, and after a final plea to the Americans to abandon ship, the lifeboat returned to St. Agnes, realising they could not return that night due to the high wind. An all-night watch was kept for distress signals but none were seen. At 2.50 a.m. with the wind at hurri-cane force, all the schooner's lights disappeared, and there was a strong smell of oil in the wind. At daybreak, the wind having moderated, the St. Agnes gig *Slippen* got across to Annet, from where the schooner could be seen bottom up on the Outer Ranneys. One man, George Allen, who was

found alive on the island, with several ribs smashed into his lungs, died soon after being taken to St. Agnes. The *Slippen* put out again in the afternoon, and two survivors, the master and engineer, were found on the southern carn of Hellweathers. The engineer was pulled into the gig by a rope, but Freddie Cook Hicks (son of the pilot lost in the wreck) had to swim ashore to assist the injured captain into the sea and out to the boat. The captain stated that when his cables parted, he had insufficient sails left to save his ship, having lost most of them in bad weather in the Atlantic crossing. Out of a crew of 18 and the pilot, only two men survived.

1908 – 20 May. *Latona*, master F. Rollo, a transatlantic liner, carrying a crew of 45, 12 cattlemen, three stowaways and four passengers, as well as a general cargo and 310 cattle, foundered 7 miles south, a half east of St. Agnes lighthouse following collision in fog with the s.s *Japanic* of Sunderland. She sank stern first without loss of human life, but all the animals drowned.
20 June. *St. Louis*, master M. Yves, a French fishing cutter of Douarnenez, was lost on the Pollard Rock, part of the Seven Stones, her crew of four being saved and landed on St. Mary's.
15 July. *Shamrock*, a 30 year old, 5-ton net barge, under tow from St. Mary's to Tresco in ballast, foundered in the Roads.

1909 – 27 February. *Volunteer*, master Parkin, a Padstow ketch for St. Mary's with slates, shipped heavy seas seven miles ESE of St. Mary's and was dismasted. Her mainmast fell on deck, smashing 30-40 feet of bulwarks, rendering her helpless. She was towed in by the *Genesta* and the steam launch *Endeavour*.
29 April. *Phyllis Anne*, a Lowestoft steam drifter, which took two very heavy seas on board in wind conditions W force 8, which started several planks, causing her to founder just west of Scilly. Her crew were saved by the Yarmouth trawler *Enterprise*.
14 August. *Plympton*, master A. Stewart, a London steamship of 2,869-tons gross, Rosario via Falmouth for Dublin with maize, struck the Lethegus Reef at 8 a.m. in dense fog. Her crew of 23 and one passenger

landed by boat on St. Agnes. That afternoon, whilst several islanders were on board engaged in the traditional pastime of 'wrecking', she suddenly slipped off the rocks without warning, turned over and partially sank, drowning Charles Hicks and Charles Mumford. Some of her cargo was saved before she disappeared.

11 October. *L'Authie*, master August Lermet, a French steam trawler of Boulogne, 198-tons gross, was lost on Gorregan in fog at 3.40 a.m, her compass and ship's log being defective. Having lost her propeller, it was impossible to get her off, and her crew of 15 landed on St. Agnes in their own boat, leaving her a total wreck.

1910 – 12 January. ***Karolos***, a Greek steamship of 2,534-tons gross, from Sulina to Londonderry developed a serious leak off Scilly and was abandoned in a sinking condition.

18 April. ***Minnehaha***, an Atlantic transport company liner of Belfast, 13,443-tons gross, New York to London with 66 passengers, a general cargo and 230 head of cattle, came in close to Shipman Head in fog, and in turning stranded on the SE side of Scilly Rock. The passengers took to the lifeboats which were guided into Great Par by the Bryher gigs *Czar* and *Sussex*. The vessel was lightened by throwing a large quantity of her cargo overboard, and the nearby coast became littered with harmoniums, cases of pens and pencils, curtain rings and rods, plaited straw, Panama hats, casks of oil, barrels of leaf tobacco, cases of 'Old Judge' cigarettes, and other valuable material, local boats putting out each morning to salvage what ever was floating around or on the rocks. The cattle were pushed overboard and towed to Samson from where they were re-shipped to Tilbury Docks. It was said that everyone from five to ninety-five was smoking the free cigarettes. Other jettisoned cargo included thousands of clocks, wringers, sewing machines, a piano and a harp. Complete motor cars in crates were towed ashore, the bottom of one crate falling out not far from Shipman Head. When recovered later the car was found to be a crumpled heap of metal! The liner was refloated on the 11th May and sailed for Falmouth under her own steam. During WW.1 she was torpedoed and sunk by the German submarine U-48 on 07.09.1917, 12 miles SE of the Fastnet Rock, with the loss of 43 lives.

22 October. *Ida*, a motor fishing vessel of St. Mary's, was lost on Little Ganinick in Crow Sound; her crew of three were saved.

1911 – 8 January. *Ardencraig*, master T. Dunning, a three- masted full-rigged ship of Glasgow, 2,153-tons gross, Melbourne to Calais with wheat, after calling at Queenstown for orders, struck the Crim in fog, floated off and about three hours later rolled over to port and foundered in the North Channel. Her crew of 31 took to their boats and were guided to St. Mary's by the St. Agnes lifeboat and a Bishop Rock lighthouse relief boat.

12 January. *Georges*, a French ketch of Auray, 80-tons net, Swansea to Trinite with coal, was abandoned in a sinking condition in St. Mary's Sound. Her crew of six reached St. Agnes in their own boat, the ketch drifting away to founder off Peninnis.

23 February. *Richelieu*. A Bishop Rock keeper reported a wreck on Retarrier Ledges amongst the Western Rocks, and in a full west gale the St. Agnes lifeboat put out to assist, and were astonished to find this French ironclad battleship on the rocks. She had been under tow from Toulon to Brest for breaking, when she parted her tow ropes and then became lost to her tugs. She drifted around the Atlantic for weeks before going ashore in Scilly, where a huge wave floated her off and she went away on the tide, later to be found by a Dutch tug. 26 March. *Setiembre*, a steamer of Bilbao, 2,171-tons gross, Porman to Maryport with iron ore, struck on Hats Ledge when entering Crow Sound for shelter. The following day she was full of water, and the crew of the salvage steamer *Lady of the Isles* were employed throwing her cargo overboard, but she became a total wreck. Her crew of 24 landed on St. Mary's.

29 March. *Buteshire*, master R. Purdie, a Glasgow barque, Pisagua to Falmouth with nitrates, was seen by the s.s *Duva* at 3 a.m, abandoned off Scilly, on fire and full of water. She was boarded, but left when it was obvious she was about to founder. Her crew left the ship 100 miles west of Brest, having toiled at her pumps for days on end, including the captain's wife, before being saved by a steamer.

4 August. *Frau Minna Petersen*, master R. May, a Norwegian schooner on passage to Hamburg with phosphate, was run down by a French steam

trawler 12 miles W of the Seven Stones. She was almost cut in two by the impact, the trawler offering to take off the crew, but said that first they had to haul in their nets. Having done this the French vessel steamed off leaving the Norwegians in their boat. The seven man crew then rowed all the way up Channel to Plymouth, landing on the Barbican Steps. Why they did not put into Penzance, Falmouth, Fowey or Looe, will never be known.

1912 – 12 March. *Wendur*, master G. H. Blackstock, a Glasgow barque of 2,046-tons gross, carrying wheat from Port Pirie to Plymouth, where she had received orders to discharge at Swansea. She struck the Seven Stones at night and filled so quickly her hatch covers were blown high in the air. Ten men got into the starboard boat and cut the falls, which then capsized. The steward drowned in the cabin and two coloured seamen refused to abandon her, so that only 18 of her crew of 21 were saved.
25 March. *Pierre L'Abbe*, master Enault, a French schooner, was sighted from Bryher burnt to the water line and drifting, and is assumed to have sunk shortly after.
11 December. *Antonios*, master T. Dambasis, a Greek steamship carrying sugar from Algiers to Liverpool. Wreckage consisting of hatch covers, an oar and the lid of a medicine chest bearing her previous name of *Greta Holme* was washed ashore on St. Agnes. Both Scilly lifeboats failed to find the wreck, which was not located until 1968 when found by divers working on the *Association*, near Old Bess Rock, her bow in 147ft/45m, on a steep slope.
26 December. *Volmer*, a Danish steamship, carrying coal from Swansea to Nice, which foundered 20 miles S of St. Mary's after developing a leak, with the loss of all 15 crew.

1913 – 17 February. *Astillero*, master M. Martinez, a Spanish steamship of Santander, carrying coal from Glasgow to Bordeaux, which foundered 20 miles N of the islands following collision with a sailing vessel. Twenty of her crew landed by the s.s *Manistree* at Liverpool, a further three by the s.s *Chindwin*.
11 June. *Toanui*, a Glasgow registered tug of 103-tons net, on passage

from the Clyde to New Zealand, believed to have sunk after striking the Seven Stones, only floating wreckage ever being found.

14 August. *Susanna*, master C. Branch, of Hamburg, a full-rigged ship, Iquique to Falmouth with nitrate and saltpetre, was lost on the Crim in fog at 11.30 p.m. Her crew of 22 took to their boats, being escorted to St. Mary's by Sennen Cove fishermen who found them near Pednathise Head.

28 November. *Thornliebank*, master G. E. Crosby, a Glasgow full-rigged ship, Pisagua to Falmouth with nitrate, struck the Crim in fog and foundered. Her crew of 25 who had taken to their boats, were in danger of drifting out to sea, but fortunately were seen by the Bishop Rock light-keepers, who called out the St. Agnes lifeboat.

1914 – 7 April. *St. Pierre*, master Andre, of Fecamp, 441-tons gross, carrying provisions and fishing gear for Newfoundland, caught fire and was abandoned five miles north of Bryher.

23 June. *Gothland*, a Red Star liner, 7,660-tons gross, from Montreal to Rotterdam with passengers, wheat and frozen meat, struck the Crim at 4.30 p.m. in fog. The passengers and most of the crew were taken off by the Scilly lifeboats, assisted by the s.s *Lyonnesse*. After a great deal of cargo had been jettisoned, she floated off on 27 June and was towed into St. Mary's Road where she was found to be sinking, and was hurriedly run aground at the southern entrance to New Grimsby Channel. There she was repaired and later towed to Southampton, but subsequently broken up.

25 July. *Lilian*, a St. Mary's fishing lugger, which foundered at the back of Annet while hauling pots in a NW gale, both crew lost.

1915 – 12 March. *Andalusian*. The first casualty of WW.1 in local waters, this Liverpool steamer of 2,349-tons gross, carrying a general cargo from her home port to Patras, was stopped by the German submarine U-29, 25 miles WNW of the Bishop Rock, her crew forced to abandon ship and her main injection valve smashed so that she filled and sank without loss of life. On the same day the s.s *Headlands* of Newcastle, carrying flints and mineral ore from Burriana to Bristol and Swansea was ordered to stop by the same submarine. Captain Lagg ignored the enemy vessel, and at 10.25 a.m. she was torpedoed eight miles S of the Bishop Rock, her crew of 23 being picked up by a patrol boat. The s.s *Lyonnesse* took her in tow and was one mile SE of the Bishop Rock when she sank The U-29 submarine claimed a third victim that day, the s.s *Indian City*, which was ordered to stop, her crew of 37 being given time to abandon ship before she was torpedoed. The enemy took the lifeboats in tow, but abandoned them when navy patrol boats appeared. By now the *Indian City* was on fire, and islanders hurried to vantage points at 7.30 a.m. as she lay 10 miles S of St. Mary's. Carrying cotton from Galveston to Le Havre, this 4,645-tons gross Bideford registered ship sank at 4.30 a.m. the following day.

30 March. *Crown of Castile*, a Glasgow steamship carrying oats and cattle fodder for France from St. John, attempted to escape from the German submarine U-28 when ordered to stop. The enemy then commenced to shell the vessel, which stopped and was abandoned, German sailors then boarding her and placed explosives. The enemy boasted to the survivors that they had sunk seven ships in four days.

1 May. Three steamships were attacked by the German submarine U-30 on the same day, causing the *Edale* of Bristol, 3,110-tons gross, carrying linseed cake from Rosario to Manchester, and the Oran registered *Europe*, 1,887-tons gross, carrying coal from Barry to St. Nazaire to sink after being torpedoed, without loss of life. The third vessel was the first American ship to be attacked during WW.1. She was the tanker *Gulflight*, master A. A. Gunther, 5,189-tons gross, torpedoed without warning 20 miles W of the Bishop. Two crew jumped overboard and drowned, the remainder being taken on board HM. mine-sweeper *Iago*. Captain Gunther died (thought to be from a heart attack), the rest of the crew, some 33-35, were taken to St. Mary's. The tanker was towed into St. Mary's Roads and temporarily repaired before continuing her voyage with a scratch crew recruited in Scilly.

27 May. *Cadeby*, a Glasgow steamship carrying pit wood, 18 crew, five passengers and a stowaway was attacked and sunk by the U-41.

2 June. *Delta B*, an Ostend fishing trawler, was sunk by gunfire from an unidentified German submarine 12 miles SSW of Scilly.

13 June. *Pelham*, a Sunderland steamship in ballast from Malta to Barry,

3,534-tons gross which was employed as an Admiralty collier No 604, was stopped by U-35, and after the crew had been allowed to escape, was sunk by scuttling charges.

3 July. *Fiery Cross*, master John Geddie, a Norwegian barque carrying oil from Philadelphia to Le Havre, was stopped by an unidentified submarine and the crew ordered to abandon ship. Her sinking by scuttling charges was delayed for 30 minutes whilst captain Geddie rowed across and demanded a receipt for his ship to prove the reason for her loss to the owners. The document read, 'I hereby certify that I have sunk the *Fiery Cross* . . . at 3 p.m. as she had contraband cargo aboard, ie. lubricating oil for France. Signed Forstman, H. Lieut.Cdr., German Imperial Marine,U-.'

31 July. Two Glasgow Admiralty fleet tenders, the s.s *Nugget*, No 38, 405-tons gross, and the *Turquoise*, No 30, 486-tons gross, both bound for the Dardanelles, were both sunk by gunfire off Scilly by the U-28.

19 August. Four vessels were lost off Scilly on the same day, three of them steamships, the *Baron Erskine*, *Restormel* and the *Samara*, all British, sunk by the German submarine U-38 by gunfire. The fourth vessel was the enemy submarine U-27, which was engrossed in getting close to the American steamship *Nicosian*, that she failed to notice another rusting vessel flying the American flag close at hand. When within 600 yards of the stranger, the American flag was replaced by a white ensign, and the tramp proved to be the Q-ship *Baralong,* armed with 12 x12pdr guns, which fired 34 shells into the submarine. Before she sank the German captain and 12 submariners swam to the abandoned *Nicosian* and attempted to climb aboard. The Q-ship opened fire on them and only four men reached her deck alive, who promptly vanished into her engine room. A party of Royal Marines went across in a boat, hunted them down and shot them dead as they were found, causing an international controversy.

21-22 August. A further four British steamships were sunk by the submarine U-38, the *Cober*; *Ruel*; *Diomen* and *Palmgrove*, all within a 40-45 mile radius of Scilly.

13 November. *Silvery Wave*, an Admiralty armed drifter, was wrecked on the eastern side of St. Mary's whilst entering Crow Sound in bad weather, HM. drifter *Boy Eddie* also going ashore, but later being refloated and saved.

1916 – 18 May. *Carbineer*, a steam trawler armed with 1 x 12pdr gun after being purchased by the Admiralty in 1915 as the *Fusilier* and re-named, struck the Crim. A Scillonian member of her crew, W. Trenear, knowing the local waters, advised her captain to put her ashore on Crebawethan Point to save lives. She became a wreck.

9 September – 24 October. A further five ships were lost by enemy action, all near the Isles of Scilly, involving the German submarine U-18. Included were the French schooner *Mysotis*, and the barque *Cannebiere*, the British steamship *Kong Ring* and the Spanish *Louis Vives*, along with the French bulk ore carrier *La Fraternite*.

13 November. *Brodfield*, master Hubert Rowland, a London steamship in ballast for Barry from Le Havre. Having navigated by dead-reckoning in fog since their last position off Start Point, Devon, she ran ashore near Blue Carn, east of Porth Minnick. Five patrol boats failed to refloat her and she became a total loss.

December. A total of five more steamships of different nationalities were lost by enemy action, many to the UC-19 and U-29 submarines, in addition to two schooners and a full-rigged ship, ranging from 10 to 35 miles from the Bishop Rock.

1917 – Between 4 January and 27 April, a further 14 merchant steamships and three sailing vessels were sunk by German submarines off the Scillies, one as close as two miles SW of the Bishop; one additional steamer, the *Don Benito*, was lost following collision. The steamers sunk by enemy action included seven Dutch vessels in one day on 22 February, out of a convoy of eight, all said to be victims of U-21, although it has been suggested they were sunk on Admiralty orders by a British subma-rine, to prevent their cargoes going on to Germany. Their names were *Bandoeng*; *Eemland*; *Gaasterland*; *Jacatra*; *Noorderdijk*; *Normanna* and *Zaandijk*. Other vessels lost included the *Ruby*, barquentine; *Airnee Maria* and *Marthe*, schooners; *Housatonic*, *Japanese Prince*, *Hesperus*, *Hunstanton*, *Penserio*, *Heather* & *Beemah*, all steamships.

13 May. *Italia*, master C. Aicario, an Italian steamer of Spezia, 2,792-tons gross, built as the *Gulf of Florida*, coal laden from Cardiff to Taranto, which went ashore on the Wingletang Ledges in fog at 3.30pm. A girl on

St.Agnes was the only witness to the wreck, but by the time she called others to the scene it had already gone down in deep water. The 23 crew landed on the island, but none of them spoke English and none of the islanders Italian, so the vessels identity remained unknown in the islands until after the war. Her 60mm stern gun was salvaged in 1964, her bell in 1976, which bore her original name still, and date of building, 1891.

14 May. *Lady Charlotte*. An Admiralty collier of 3,593-tons gross, carrying coal from Cardiff to Alexandria, stranded in dense fog during the same night as the *Italia*, going ashore on the rocks at the mouth of Porth Hellick. Crew all saved.

27 May. An unidentified German submarine was bombed and sunk off Scilly, by a flying boat from RNAS. Tresco.

31 May. *Jeanne Cordonnier*, a French barque of 2,194-tons gross, carrying nitrate from Iquique to Le Havre, was torpedoed by a German submarine, the survivors being adrift in open boats for 39 hours before being saved by the St. Agnes lifeboat.

9 June. *Mar Cor*, a Genoese steamship carrying coal, was stopped by the German submarine UB-32 and her crew forced to abandon ship, after which she was torpedoed 25 miles west of the Bishop.

12 June. *South Point*, master D. J. Bowen, a London registered steamship of 4,258-tons gross in ballast to Newport News, torpedoed in convoy by the submarine UB-32, SW of the Bishop.

15 June. *Albertine Beatrice*, a Dutch sailing vessel carrying a cargo of tobacco from Surabaya, foundered SW of Scilly in a gale.

28 August. *Beechpark*, a Newcastle collier, carrying coal and coke from the Tyne to Port Said, torpedoed by the German submarine UC-75 four miles S of St. Mary's.

25 August. *Nascent*, an armed steamship of Sunderland, carrying a general cargo from Tegal and Dakar for Hull, which was torpedoed by the submarine UC-49, 20 miles SSW of the Bishop, three men being killed in the engine room, a further three drowning.

4 September. *Sadi Carnot*, a French sailing ship of 354-tons gross, sunk by a German submarine which placed scuttling charges.

3 October. *Annie F. Conlon*, an American three-masted schooner, which had several shells fired into her hull by a German submarine 12 miles SE

of St. Mary's, which was towed into Crow Sound on the 5th, and run ashore on Southward Ledge, near St. Martin's. Here 466 drums of lubricating oil were recovered as the wreck broke up.

18 October. *Madura*, master W. Ferguson, an armed merchant steamship of Glasgow, 4,484-tons gross, carrying a general cargo from Sydney for France. She was torpedoed by the submarine U-62, 23 miles WSW of the Bishop, three of her crew being killed.

22 October. *Eastgate*, a London steamship, 4,277-tons gross, torpedoed whilst in convoy for the USA, was towed in and beached near Nut Rock before being taken away for repairs. Part of her cargo consisted of French perfume, and it has been said that every person in the islands seemed to have an exquisite aroma similar to a flower garden for years afterwards!

6 December. USS. *Jacob Jones*, an American four-funnelled destroyer, escorting a convoy off Queenstown, was carrying out target shooting practice with the USS. *Nicholson*, which attracted the attention of a German submarine, which got to within 800 yards without detection, then sunk the *Jacob Jones* with a single torpedo 25 miles SW of the Bishop. As she went down all the depth-charges already primed for instant use exploded, killing 64 of her crew.

28 December. *Seapoint*, a London steamship from Newport for Rouen with coal, sprang a leak and sank near the Seven Stones.

1918 – 14 March. *A.A. Raven*, an American coal laden steamship of Philadelphia, torpedoed by a German submarine 17 miles SE of St. Mary's.

24 July. HMS *Pincher*, a destroyer of 905-tons gross, carrying a crew of 96, wrecked on the Seven Stones in fog.

7 September. *Rio Mondego*, a Portuguese schooner of 733-tons gross, Setubal to Swansea with wine, was towed in and beached near Stoney Island having been shelled by an enemy submarine on 1st September and abandoned. Despite a caretaker on board, sailors from RNAS. Tresco flying boat base managed to salvage a considerable amount of wine for their own use.

30 September. *Atlantico*, a Portuguese schooner of Oporto, coal laden from Newport, was sunk by gunfire from a submarine. Her crew reached

Broad Sound in their boat, where a Bishop Rock keeper saw them and called out the St. Agnes lifeboat. After landing six men, five of whom were injured, a second boat was found with three more survivors.

10 November. HMS. *Blazer*, a requisitioned tug, used as an examination vessel, was returning from Penzance having heard news that an armistice meant that WW.1 was over. She got inside the Woolpack and struck near the Steval where she sank. Half her crew escaped in the ship's boat, the remainder were picked up by J. Pender, using Admiralty Trot boat No 9 based at St. Mary's.

1919 – 27 November. *Marion G. Douglas*, an American three-masted schooner, 491-tons gross, was discovered abandoned in Hell Bay by Bryher men. They boarded and sailed her into St. Mary's Road, the vessel later being towed to Glasgow. She had been abandoned on the American side of the Atlantic, and it was thought this was an insurance fraud since the crew said she was sinking when they left her, whereas she was almost dry when found in Scilly.

1920 – 11 May. *Gladys*, a St. Mary's crabber, manned by two sons of the lifeboat coxswain, is believed to have been lost on Great Smith. The St. Mary's lifeboat *Elsie* put out and searched, but returned empty handed.

6 September. *Homestead*, a Newcastle steamship carrying coal from Blyth to Cork, foundered in heavy seas at 2.30 a.m. after developing a huge leak. Her crew spent four hours in their open boat before being picked up by a French crabber and landed at St. Ives.

25 November. *Zenith*, master H. Wetherall, foundered between the Isles of Scilly and Wolf Rock, crew saved in their own boat.

2 December. *Hathor*, master Sievers, a German steamship interned in a Chilian port at the outbreak of WW.1, which suffered five years neglect at anchor before being released following the armistice. She sailed for Portland with a cargo of nitrate, but broke down off the Azores. Picked up by two tugs and taken in tow, she broke adrift SW of Scilly, and drove ashore on Lethegus Rocks, St. Agnes. The St. Mary's lifeboat *Elsie* went out and in a difficult and dangerous operation, seas being 30 feet high, she managed to save all 24 crew.

1921 – 20 January. HMS. **K-5**, Commander Alan Poland RN, one of the infamous 'K-Class' steam,diesel,electric driven submarines, laid down in 1915 as submersible destroyers. At the time they were the largest, heaviest and fastest submarines in the world. Engaged in a mock battle with British surface warships and four other 'K' boats off Scilly, **K-5** failed to surface, and was posted as 'missing' with all fifty-seven crew in 49N, 9W, some 100 miles SW of the Bishop Rock. Wooden floor-boards from the control room, bearing the numbers of the battery cells they covered, a large quantity of oil, and the lid of a torpedo gunners' mate's ditty box bearing a name were later found on the surface. The reason for her loss will never be known, since the wreck, which has never been found, lies in a depth of between 600ft and 12,000ft of water.

2 February. **Leon Bonnat**, master Robert Chaique, Cardiff for Bayonne with coal, struck the Crim having sprung a leak earlier. The water in her hold was almost level with her deck and she sank in five minutes. The Bishop Rock keepers called out the St. Mary's lifeboat **Elsie**, which saved all twelve crew.

11 July. **Western Front**, master Richard O'Brien, a 5,743-gross ton American steamer carrying a cargo of turpentine and naptha, which caught fire 20 miles west of the Bishop. Following a hugh explosion she became engulfed in flames from bow to stern and was abandoned. Her crew were saved by the s.s **British Earl** and the St. Mary's lifeboat **Elsie**, which reported her as sinking seven miles WSW of the Bishop, although the master stated 20 miles west.

1922 – March. **Optimist**, a 130-tons gross, three-masted schooner, which was lost off Scilly.

1925 – 20 January. HMS **Monarch**, a Dreadnought battleship of the **Orion** class, 22,500-tons, armed with 10 x 13.5ins and 16 x 4ins guns, 545 feet long, was scuttled as a target off the Isles of Scilly for underwater detection trials by the Royal Navy.

22 March. **Cite de Verdun**, a steam trawler of Boulogne, 214-tons gross, was lost on Rosevear at midnight during a snow storm. Her crew of 30 was rescued by the St. Mary's lifeboat **Elsie**.

1926 – 9 January. *Miarka*, a coal laden French schooner of Rochelle, sank off St. Mary's following collision.

30 May. *Keyes*, a steam trawler of Lowestoft (LT-580), arrived at St. Mary's that evening having struck a reef near St. Martin's in fog.

1927 – 27 October. *Isabo*, master Tarabocchia, of Lussin-Piccolo, laden with grain in bulk from Montreal to Hamburg, went ashore on Scilly Rock in fog and became a total loss. Twenty-eight of the crew of thirty-eight were saved by Bryher men, using the boats *Sunbeam*, *Czar* and *Ivy*, leaving the St. Mary's lifeboat *Elsie* to save four men left clinging to her foremast. 2nd coxn. J. T. Lethbridge, received the RNLI bronze medal for bravery and devotion to duty for this rescue.

23 December. *Gougou*, master Morbihan, a French schooner with a crew of seven, was dismasted off Scilly and abandoned, her crew being saved by the St. Mary's lifeboat *Elsie*. Tugs were sent to search for her, but she was found by the Trinity steamer *Mermaid* and towed to Penzance.

26 December. *Lady Daphne*, a Thames barge of Rochester, 88-tons net, from the Thames to Plymouth with bricks and tiles, was abandoned off the Lizard at 7 a.m. and drifted all the way to Skirt Island, where she went ashore at 2.15 p.m, sinking during the night. The master had been washed overboard and drowned when off Plymouth, and the Lizard lifeboat took off her two man crew. The St. Mary's lifeboat *Elsie* and a launch belonging to the Duchy of Cornwall were able to beach the wreck inside the Old Quay at 10 a.m. on the 29th , for which they received a salvage award of £580. The only life on board the barge was a caged canary.

1929 – 20 March. *Lord Haldane*, master Bridge, a 91-tons gross Lowestoft steam drifter, struck Steval rock at 5 a.m. in fog, being refloated at 9.10 a.m. assisted by the St. Mary's lifeboat *Elsie*.

1931 – 28 June. *Oakwold*, a Grimsby trawler, struck a rock near Scilly in dense fog during the night. Badly damaged and leaking she was escorted to Plymouth by a sister trawler, arriving safely.

7 October. *Horsham*, a small steamer of Guernsey, proceeding from St. Mary's to Tresco, struck a rock in New Grimsby Channel, and after temporary repair sailed for Par, Cornwall.

1932 – 12 April. *Yvonne et Marie*, a French fishing vessel (CM-2025) stranded at night on a ledge in Tresco Channel, and efforts by the lifeboat to refloat her were unsuccessful. She was finally got afloat by the St. Mary's lifeboat *Cunard* and taken into St. Mary's leaking.
5 August. *Scillonian*, the islands mail steamer, stranded on Bacon Ledge at 1.30 p.m. in dense fog and remained there for an hour and a half. Some 200 passengers were landed by the local boats *White Hope*, *Gugh* and some barges. The first of these laid out a kedge anchor and 120 fathoms of 6 inch manilla, which assisted her to be refloated without damage.

1933 – 11 May. A motor boat belonging to the French crabber *Korriguan* (CM-2421) was totally lost on Mincarlo. After spending all night on the island, the four occupants, two from the *Korriguan* and two from the *Henri Lucia* (CM-2429) were rescued by the St. Mary's lifeboat *Cunard*. nb. The *Henri Lucia* went aground on Tresco on 26 January 1935, but was refloated the same day having suffered only the loss of her punt.

1936 – 2 April. *Christianborg*. Land's End Radio received a distress signal at 9.10 p.m. from this steamship, saying that she was aground in the Isles of Scilly in position 49.44N; 06.27W, but was in no immediate danger. At 11.44 p.m. she reported she was afloat and proceeding.

1939 – 6 December. *Britta*, a Norwegian motor tanker of 6,214-tons, was torpedoed by the submarine U-47 (Capt. Prien) at 8.29 p.m, in 49.48N; 06.51W, 22 miles off Scilly, the tanker sinking after a huge explosion which killed six of her thirty-one crew.
22 December. *Longships*, a Glasgow steamer of 1,562-tons gross, Belfast to Plymouth with a general cargo, struck the Seven Stones in fog where she broke her back. Her crew of 27 were saved by the St. Mary's lifeboat *Cunard*, and given breakfast at the Pier Cafe, before leaving on the Scillonian for Penzance.

1942 – 5 May. *Scillonian*, on entering St. Mary's at 12.30 p.m. in fog, stranded on Newford Island, and remained there with a list to starboard until 8 p.m, when she was refloated without damage.

8 August. *Ngaroma*, a South African steamship was lost without trace on the Seven Stones.

1943 – 10 January. An un-named trawler, believed to have been a Government vessel engaged in secret agent landings on the coast of France, struck Bacon Ledge when entering St. Mary's in a southerly gale. She sank close to the quay after the crew had been taken off.
14 November. *LCT-354*. Five British tank landing craft put into Porthmellon at 8 p.m, four of which beached in safety, but the fifth went ashore on the rocks of Newford Island, remaining high and dry as the tide fell. The barges had come from Gibraltar, taking nine days due to storms, 22 others turning up elsewhere, returning to the UK from Crete, North Africa, Sicilly and Salerno, ready for the D-Day Normandy landings. With 16-18 men on board each barge, only two were lost overboard on passage. *LCT-354* was refloated next day with the assistance of Lieut. R. Chudleigh (once of Tresco) sent over from Falmouth as a salvage expert, and the local fire service.

1945 – 24 February. An RAF. Sunderland flying-boat landed shortly before dawn and tore open her hull on the Pots. Her crew were taken off before she drifted onto Mare Ledges where she was lost. On the same day the German submarine *U-480*, Oberleutnant zur See Hans Joachim Forster, a VIIIC class vessel and the first U-Boat fitted with a schnorkel, was attacked and sunk with all hands by HM frigates *Rowly* and *Duckworth* using depth charges, after a six hour attack, 7.25 miles SE of Deep Point, St. Mary's.
11 March. *U-681*, Oberleutnant zur See Werner Gebauer, a German type V11C submarine, carrying a crew of 38, ran aground while attempting to enter St. Mary's Roads to attack shipping. At 11 a.m, when at 80 feet depth, she struck a rock and damaged her hull and propellers. With water pouring into her engine and control rooms, she was forced to surface, at which point her captain attempted to escape the area on the surface, heading for Ireland, 130 miles away. She was spotted by a Liberator bomber of 103 squadron, US. Navy, from carrier VP-103. The pilot, Lieut. Field, made two attacks, dropping eight depth charges on the second run, badly

damaging the enemy vessel forcing her crew to abandon. The enemy climbed into the dinghies, while demolition charges were set and her main vents opened. An escort vessel was sent to pick up the crew. It has been said that the U-681 sank in Broad Sound, since a party of islanders were on a pleasure trip amongst the Western Rocks when the Liberator passed overhead, at which the islanders gaily waved, which changed to surprise, when a stick of depth charges were dropped into the sea.

1946 – 20 September. *Noel*, a French crabber which capsized off Scilly during a storm and sank almost immediately. One of the crew was lost, the remaining five taking to their dinghy but were not rescued until twenty-four hours later.

1949 – 6 October. *Fantee*, a motor vessel of Liverpool, 6,369-tons gross, from Matadi and Amsterdam to Liverpool, with hardwood logs, ground nuts, palm oil, cocoa, and other general cargo, was lost in fog on the Seven Stones. Her crew of 53 got away in two boats, and were picked up by the Scillonian launches, *Kittern* and *Golden Spray*. Logs from her cargo are still being salvaged and used for making furniture and general joinery work on St. Mary's.

1952 – Summer. Two men put out from Scilly to retrieve fishing gear from near the Crim, but a huge wave broke over them and neither the men nor their boat were ever seen again.

1955 – 21 January. *Mando*, master Syras Svoronoss, a Panamanian motor vessel, built as a US. Liberty ship *Stepas Darius*, carrying 9,000 tons of coal from Hampton Roads to Rotterdam, struck on Golden Ball Bar at 8.30 p.m. in fog after suffering an engine breakdown when 120 miles west of Scilly. The St. Mary" lifeboat *Cunard*, since it was low water, had to grope her way past Southward Wells, up through the Norrad Rocks and round Shipman Head to reach her. The crew lowered two boats, the lifeboat then taking them all on board, and with the boats in tow set off for St. Mary's, picking up the Bryher gig *Sussex* on the way, this being the last time a gig was engaged in rescue work. The Italian cook of the

Mando, had been a pantry-boy on board the *Isabo*, lost on Scilly Rock in 1927.

22 July. *Punta*, master Angelos Mathiassos, of Panama, 2,197-tons gross, Bougie for Portishead Dock with phosphate rock, was lost on the Seven Stones in fog. Her crew of 22, the master's wife, two Somali stowaways, one cat, two kittens, two linnets, a canary and a goldfinch were all landed at St. Mary's by the lifeboat *Cunard*.

August. *White Hope*, a St. Mary's motor launch, went ashore at Carn Near and became a total loss. She was uninsured.

1958 – 2 April. *Jeanne Francoise*. A body and the wreck of this yacht was discovered on Crebawethan. She had sailed from Le Croisie for Harfleur on 21 March with a crew consisting of father and son. A fierce SE gale sprang up during the night, and the yacht was never seen again. The body of the father was later picked up on the south coast of Ireland.

1959 – October. Five men returning from Tresco after a day's work there had a narrow escape when their boat sank. The punt drifted ashore on Tresco and was dashed to pieces.

26 December. The motor launch *Mayflower* belonging to the Isles of Scilly S.S. Co. broke down when leaving St. Mary's harbour for Tresco in a heavy ground sea. She drove onto Newford Island where she was holed and filled with water, but her passengers and crew were saved.

1960 – 31 December. *Indian Navigator*, an Indian steamship of 7,660-tons gross, registered at Calcutta and carrying sulphur from Hamburg and Liverpool to her home port, suffered a violent explosion in No 4 and 5 holds. A serious fire was started which spread to the accommodation, and she was abandoned burning approximately 40 miles south of Scilly. A sister ship, the *Indian Success* put a salvage party on board, hoping to put out the fire and tow her to the nearest port. There was then a second, unexpected explosion and the *Indian Navigator* suddenly sank, taking with her all 18 in the salvage party.

1961 – February. A barge belonging to the Isle of Scilly S.S. Co. broke free from St. Mary's Quay in a gale and was wrecked.

The super-tanker *Torrey Canyon* went ashore on the Pollard Rock,
Seven Stones, on 18 March 1967. Broken in three by the sea, she was bombed and her
oil cargo set on fire, the largest and most environmentaly damaging of all the shipwrecks
around Gt. Britain.

Acknowledgment: Frank Gibson

26 April. A cabin cruiser was torn from her moorings at Tresco in a gale and wrecked on the rocks.

1962 – Mid-January. Three foreign fishing vessels were lost in bad weather. Wreckage from one of them, the French trawler *Le Matelot*, was washed ashore on Scilly.

1965 – 4 August. *Louison Bobet*, a French fishing vessel, struck a submerged object, possibly one of the Eastern Isles rocks and sank within 45 minutes.

1966 – November. The St. Mary's lifeboat *Guy & Clare Hunter*, was called out to deal with – a cockroach! The Indian cargo vessel *Akbar Jayanti*, radioed for medical assistance for a seaman with a distressing complaint – a cockroach had entered his ear and all attempts to extricate it had made the insect swell up. Doctor D. W. Bell, of St. Mary's boarded from the lifeboat, and soon had the insect removed. He later commented, 'When this type of insect gets into the human ear, it can drive people mad.'

1967 – 18 March. *Torrey Canyon*, master Rugiati Pastrengo, a Liberian registered super tanker, 61,236-tons gross, carrying 119,328-tons of crude oil, was wrecked on the Pollard Rock, Seven Stones at 8.40 a.m, in fine clear weather conditions. She was steaming north at 16 knots for Milford Haven on automatic pilot, when she struck, no one on board having noticed the Seven Stones lightship, its warning rockets, or international flag hoist of 'JD' which indicated she was standing into danger. The Dutch salvage tug *Utrecht* made three attempts to refloat her, and the wreck survived two gales and an internal explosion before breaking her back. The resultant oil spill was the first such major incident in the world, fouling beaches in Cornwall and Devon, but fortunately not the Isles of Scilly. On 28 March, with the ship in three pieces, she was bombed and the oil set on fire, in an attempt to reduce pollution. In February 1982 her forepart was raised intact and converted into an oil storage barge. This is still the largest total wreck in British waters.

1968 – September. *Regency*, master William Sutton, a converted American mine-sweeper of 150-tons, described as a survey/salvage vessel, chartered by a London syndicate to support divers on the wreck of the *Association*, foundered off the Wolf Rock whilst returning to Penzance. Her crew of nine saved themselves in inflatables.

13 October. *Salvor*, a small ex-government LC(P)[Landing Craft, Personnel] engaged in diving work around the islands and on the wreck of the *Association*, capsized in heavy seas and sank near the entrance to Crow Sound. Her crew took to their inflatable and were picked up by a launch from St. Mary's.

1970 – 24 February. *Jean Gougy*, a Fecamp registered, French motor fishing vessel of 246-tons gross. The body of her chief engineer was found ashore at New Grimsby, raising fears that she may have sunk, the serial number on the lifejacket worn by the corpse (D.1714) being positively identified by the owners. The wreck was not found until August that year when it was seen on the seabed off Pednathise Head. The trawler had called at Newlyn on 19.02 to land the mate who had injured an arm. She was expected to call back two days later to pick him up, but nothing was heard from her or her 14 man crew from 8 p.m. on 21.02, when she passed a radio message saying she was 25 miles west of Bishop Rock.

15 April. *Poleire*, master Coulouris Gerasimos, a Famagusta registered Cypriot motor vessel, carrying zinc concentrate from Foynes to Gdynia with a crew of 15. Navigating past Scilly in fog by radio beacon only, her radar being unserviceable, Shipman Head was seen to starboard and her engine stopped, but she struck the rocks off Gimble Point, Tresco on Little Kettle Rock, and became a total wreck. Her Mayday distress call gave a position much nearer the Bishop Rock, and although the St. Mary's lifeboat *Guy & Clare Hunter*, was launched at 4.43 a.m, having been given an incorrect location did not arrive alongside until 6.35am. In the meantime, the Bryher launch *Faldore* had found the wreck and taken off her crew.

1971 – 19 December. *Tralee Trader*, a Panamanian motor vessel of 499-tons gross, on passage from Rotterdam to Cork, foundered after suffering a shift of cargo in heavy weather seven miles NE of the Seven Stones.

1972 – 16 January. *Bernard de Percin*, a French motor fishing vessel of L'Orient, 143-tons gross, put out a distress call at 11.55 p.m. saying she was taking in a lot of water. Her crew were rescued and the vessel taken in tow by another French trawler *Armide*, but when the tow rope parted she was so low in the water she was abandoned to sink.

1973 – 24 April. *Richard Davey*, a 30ft sailing ketch, burst into flames whilst at anchor in New Grimsby Harbour. She was towed ashore and beached, but burnt out completely, with the death of one of her two crew.

1974 – 16 January. *Kingfisher*, a 30ft St. Agnes owned fishing boat, sank at her moorings during a severe gale. Several small boats were also lost.

1975 – 1 August. *Venus de Isles*, master Goddard, a motor fishing vessel, developed a leak, the St. Mary's lifeboat *Guy & Clare Hunter*, saving the crew and taking the vessel in tow until she sank.

1976 – March. *Saphhrin*, a Swiss yacht with a crew of six, bound from Oessant Island for Scilly disappeared. There was no clue as to her fate until July that year, when wreckage identified as coming from the yacht was found on Crebawethan.
26 September. *Rarau*, a Romanian fish factory vessel, of 2,681-tons gross, stranded on the Seven Stones early in the morning. Her crew of 84 were rescued after taking to the ship's lifeboats and rafts. She subsequently broke her back and foundered.
14 October. *Grey Ghost*, a St. Mary's motor boat, used to take out diving parties, broke from her moorings and drove ashore at Porthmellon, where she became a total loss.
15 November. The St. Mary's lifeboat *Guy & Clare Hunter*, rescued nine persons from a motor boat which sank at night at the entrance to St. Mary's Harbour.

1977 – 13 February. *Enfant de Bretagne*, of St. Malo, a motor fishing vessel of 50-tons net, was lost during the early hours with all five crew in the narrow stretch of water between the north-east side of Pednathise

Head and adjacent rocks. The St. Mary's lifeboat *Guy & Clare Hunter*, was launched at 2.15 am. with Matt Lethbridge as cox'n, and using parachute flares, searched the very worst areas of the Western Rocks in total darkness and a heavy swell. Shouts were heard from the rocks, and the lifeboat's search light picked out the bow of the wreck 25ft up on the rocks, but with no signs of life. A helicopter from RNAS. Culdrose recovered one body, the lifeboat a second. For that service, the cox'n received his third silver medal and his six crewmen thanks of the Institution on vellum.

1979 – 14 August. Around noon, the Bishop Rock keepers reported a yacht sinking south of Scilly. When a SAR helicopter arrived 30 minutes later the yacht had disappeared, and is believed to have been one of the five Fastnet Challenge Cup competitors considered 'lost, believed sunk' during a SW force 10 storm.
16 September. *Marie des Isles*, a 58ft Breton crabber, drifted on to Innisidgen during the early hours, heeled over on the afternoon tide and sank. She was later raised and towed to St. Mary's quay.

1980 – 17 March. *Le Resolu*, a French wooden side-trawler of Guilvinec, 48-tons gross, was reported in distress on the Seven Stones at about midnight. Wreckage found two weeks later, one mile south of Tater Du light, near Land's End, matched her description, and it is believed she either struck the Seven Stones or was run down by another vessel. Her five man crew was lost.

1982 – 14 May. *Pathfinder*, skipper Michael Mahon, a 71ft mfv of Newlyn, foundered after colliding with the Sudanese vessel *L. Obeid* off the Bishop Rock.

1983 – 16 July. Having left the Penzance heliport at 11.20am. after poor visibility had delayed schedules, a routine S-61 Sikorsky helicopter(G-BEON) flight to St.Mary's reduced its height from 2,000 to 500ft on approaching the islands, where it again encountered fog. Permission was given by the air traffic controller for the aircraft to make its final approach at 250ft height, but when still two miles out it flew into the sea, rolled over and sank in 200ft of water. Of the twenty-three passengers, two pilots and a cabin attendant on board, only six survived.These included the pilots and four passengers(two of whom were islanders). A relief St.Mary's lifeboat, the *Sir Max Aitken*, put to sea under Cox'n Matt Lethbridge, and found the survivors who by now had been in the water for over an hour. Those who lost their lives included an entire family of holiday makers. The helicopter was later salvaged by the Royal Navy, landed at Falmouth, then taken on to RAE. Farnborough for examination by the DOT's. Accidents Investigation Branch. The inquiry into the accident found it had been caused by a combination of pilot error, deceptive weather conditions over calm seas, insufficient company operating procedures and the lack of audio height warning equipment. Both pilots were praised for their courage and determination in assisting the four surviving passengers to stay afloat, as were the crew of the St.Mary's lifeboat for its timely despatch and their skill in locating the survivors.

3 September. A new boat, of which David Peacock was part owner, broke from her moorings at Perconger in a NW gale and drove ashore on the Gugh, St. Agnes, where she broke up.

1986 – 25 June. *Ubiquitous*, a Drascombe lugger, was sighted bottom up a mile off St. Martin's, her crew of two presumably having drowned.

1993 – 12 September. The yacht *Baracole*, was smashed to pieces in Porthcressa. The St.Mary's lifeboat *Robert Edgar* rescued one man. The rescue was featured in a BBC. '999' series TV. programme.

1996 – 15 August. *Flem Art*, a Falmouth registered fishing vessel (FH-138), 20.65-tons gross, built in 1976, sank after grounding in Crow Channel at 3.14 a.m. The vessel was later raised and moved to Porthloo, since it lay in the navigational channel.From there it was taken alongside St. Mary's quay for an insurance survey, before repair and towage back to Newlyn.

1997 – 26 March. *Cita*, master Jerzy Wojtkow, a feeder container ship of 3,083-tonnes gross, from Southampton to Belfast with a general cargo, drove ashore at full speed on a reef of rocks at Porth Hellick at 3.30 a.m, with only one man on the bridge who was fast asleep, the ship on automatic pilot, and the radar warning alarm turned off. The St. Mary's lifeboat *Robert Edgar*, was called out at 4 a.m. and had already rescued six crew members, when an SAR helicopter from RNAS. Culdrose arrived to lift off the one remaining injured crewman, who was then lowered to the lifeboat. At daybreak, the rocks and beaches from Porthcressa to Porth Hellick were seen to be littered with steel containers, some intact, others hanging open spilling cargo. With such a varied range of goods now washing around in the shallows, or else on the rocks for the taking, the Scillonians took part in the best salvage bonanza ever experienced in the islands, better even than the s.s *Minnehaha* in 1910. As well as £1m worth of tobacco, she carried clothing, shoes, vehicle tyres, forklift trucks, shopping bags, refuse sacks, sport trophies, wooden flooring and hardwood doors, batteries, power tools, toys, car and lorry spares, gas cylinders, clothing, shoes, barbecue sets, bathroom accessories, kitchen scales, towels, chemicals, golf bags, even gravestones, and many other items, all of which the islanders made good use of. Surplus clothing was collected, washed, bundled and sent to Romanian childrens homes.

17 May. *Albatros*, a 24,804-tonnes gross Nassau registered, ex-Cunard cruise-liner, struck the North Bartholomew Ledge in St.Mary's Sound, at 3.05pm. Carrying over 500 mainly elderly German passengers, after a brief stay in the Roads she sailed for the Isle of Wight, but in leaving tore a 131ft(40m) hole in her starboard side and returned to anchor The island's Council Crisis Management team went to 'red-alert,' and the Coastguard Agency's Marine Pollution Unit flew to Scilly for the second time in six weeks. Anticipating a potentially catastrophic oil spill of the 480-tonnes of bunkers carried, fortunately pollution was minimal, her fuel oil being safely pumped into the coastal tanker *Falmouth Endeavour*, placed alongside. Her passengers were disembarked and taken to Penzance on board the *Scillonian III*, where they were met by a fleet of seventeen buses, which transported them and their luggage to London. The *Albatross*, with a salvage tug in attendance, later proceeded to Southampton under her own power for dry-docking, inspection and repair.

Index

Cober........................1915
Colossus...................1798
Comet........................1828
Conquerant...............1781
Cornelia....................1861
Cornish Girl.............1873
Courier.....................1808
Craig Elvan..............1898
Craven......................1757
Criccieth Castle.........1883
Crown of
    Castile 1915
Cubana......................1866
Cubana......................1888
Culmore....................1881
Custos........................1856
Dauphine..................1866
David.........................1867
Decoy........................1904
Defiance....................1844
Delaware..................1871
Delta B......................1915
Diamond....................1855
Diana.........................1738
Diligence..................1740
Diligente...................1694
Diligente...................1858
Diomen......................1915
Dispatch....................1812
Don Benito...............1917
Douglas.....................1771
Douro........................1843
Dover........................1667
Dowson.....................1787
Draper 1745
Duchess of
    Leinster..............1768
Duck...........................1807
Duke of
    Cornwall...........1787
Duke of
    Cumbereland..........1764

Duke of
    Cumberland..........1773
Duke of
    Cumberland..........1776
Duke of
    Wellington 1859
Eagle 1707
Eagle 1764
Eagle 1790
Eagle 1848
Earl of Arran.............1872
Earl of
    Lonsdale 1885
Eastgate....................1917
Edale 1915
Eddystone.................1846
Eemland 1917
Elaine 1876
Eliza 1817
Eliza 1818
Eliza 1866
Eliza 1891
Elizabeth 1757
Elizabeth 1786
Elizabeth 1790
Elizabeth 1825
Elizabeth 1852
Elizabeth 1873
Elizabeth Line...........1774
Elspeth 1857
Embiricos 1892
Emilie........................1866
Emma........................1843
Empire.......................1860
Endeavour 1666
Endeavour 1737
Endeavour 1781
Enfant de
    Bretagne 1977
E.R.I. 1871
Erne
    Hagemeister..........1861

Erik Rickmers...........1899
Esperance 1801
Essie.........................1877
Euphemie 1863
Europa......................1763
Europe......................1915
Excelsior 1881
Expedition 1766
Expedition 1785
Express......................1869
Factory Girl..............1863
Falkland 1901
Fame.........................1836
Fame.........................1858
Famiglia
    Cavallo..........1904
Fanny 1820
Fanny 1872
Fantee.......................1949
Felicity 1773
Felix Guemole 1889
Fiery Cross...............1915
Financier 1783
Firebrand 1707
Flink 1867
Floresta.....................1875
Flossie 1880
Fly 1837
Flying Fish................1736
Fortuna......................1809
Fortune 1759
Fortune 1802
Francisco...................1802
Francisco...................1811
Frau Minna
    Peterson...........1911
Freden 1796
Frederick 1877
Fredericus.................1783
Frere et Soeur...........1891
Friar Tuck................1863
Friendship 1758

Pierre L'Abbe 1912
Pincher 1918
Plato 1892
Plenty 1840
Plump 1885
Plympton 1909
Poleire 1970
Porth 1891
Pownall 1759
Pretty Peggy 1759
Prima 1828
Primos 1871
Primrose 1654
Prinses Maria 1686
Prosper 1829
Prosperous 1836
Providence 1755
Providence 1833
Providence 1854
Providencia 1821
Providentia
          Divina 1782
Punjab 1860
Punta 1955
Quatre Freres et
          Marie 1868
Queen 1880
Queen Charlotte 1815
Quicksilver 1804
Rapid 1860
Rarau 1976
Recovery 1795
Regency 1968
Restormel 1915
Revenge 1674
Reward 1810
Richard Warbrick 1882
Richard Davey 1973
Rio Mondego 1918
River Lune 1879
Robert & Sally 1784
Romney 1707

Rosaire 1879
Rosa Tacchini 1872
Rosherville 1855
Roxburgh Castle 1891
Royal James 1650
Royal Oak 1665
Ruby 1917
Ruel 1915
Ruperra 1903
Sackville 1832
Sadi Carnot 1917
Sado 1870
St.Antonio de
          Lisboa 1781
St.Christophe 1907
St.Jean 1880
St.Joseph 1739
St.Louis 1908
St.Peterburg 1870
St.Pierre 1914
St.Vincent 1839
St.Vincent 1882
Sally 1769
Sally 1819
Salmon 1871
Salvor 1968
Samara 1915
San Giorgio 1851
Saphhrin 1976
Sarah 1853
Sarah 1865
Sarah 1870
Sarah & Emma 1863
Schiller 1875
Scipio 1758
Scotia 1863
Sea Flower 1748
Sea Horse 1766
Seapoint 1917
Seinte Marie
     de Coronade 1354
Serica 1893

Setiembre 1911
Shamrock 1908
Shannon 1820
Sidonie 1825
Signora Carmina 1807
Silvery Wave 1915
Sisters 1801
Solace 1839
Sophie 1896
South Point 1917
Squirrel 1773
Speedwell 1759
Stormont 1790
Sultana 1853
Sultana 1895
Supply 1617
Susan 1827
Susanna 1741
Susanna 1913
Susannah 1817
Sussex 1885
Swallow 1807
Swann 1639
Symmetry 1840
Tamar 1807
Tancred 1848
Tartar 1779
Terwagout 1788
Thames 1841
Thelma 1748
Theodorick 1839
Theris 1779
Thomas 1776
Thomas & Sally 1812
Thomas &
          William 1801
Thomas W.
          Lawson 1907
Thornliebank 1913
Three Sisters 1777
Ticina 1869
Toanui 1913

142